SIGNS & WONDERS

A REFORMED LOOK AT
THE SPIRIT'S ONGOING WORK

JOHN A. ALGERA

FAITH
ALIVE®
Christian Resources

Grand Rapids, Michigan

Signs and Wonders: A Reformed Look at the Spirit's Ongoing Work, © 2006 by Faith Alive Christian Resources, 2850 Kalamazoo Ave. SE, Grand Rapids, MI 49560. All rights reserved. With the exception of brief excerpts for review purposes, no part of this book may be reproduced in any manner whatsoever without written permission from the publisher. Printed in the United States of America on recycled paper.

We welcome your comments. Call us at 1-800-333-8300, or e-mail us at editors@faithaliveresources.org.

Library of Congress Cataloging-in-Publication Data
Algera, John A.
Signs and wonders: a reformed look at the spirit's ongoing work / John A. Algera.
p. cm.
Includes bibliographical references.
ISBN 1-59255-291-9 (alk. paper)
1. Holy Spirit. 2. Miracles. 3. Gifts, Spiritual. 4. Reformed Church—Doctrines.
I. Title.
BT121.3.A44 2006
234'.13—dc22
                                2006016810

10 9 8 7 6 5 4 3 2 1

TO DEBRA JOY

"Now, Lord, consider their threats and enable your servants to speak your word with great boldness. Stretch out your hand to heal and perform miraculous signs and wonders through the name of your holy servant Jesus."

—Acts 4:29-30

ACKNOWLEDGMENTS

First of all, I thank my congregation at Madison Avenue Christian Reformed Church in Paterson, New Jersey, for their faithful support and for their love and care for me and my family over 27 years of ministry together. I am grateful for the study leaves they granted me to work on this topic for my doctoral thesis, and for a recent two-month sabbatical. I am thankful for those who tested this material when it was first taught as an adult course and for their openness to learn with me. I am continually surprised at God's work and how God uses people, through the love of Jesus and the power of the Holy Spirit, to teach one another.

Second, I wish to thank Christian Reformed Home Missions for their sponsorship of the "Kingdom Power and Evangelism" conference in 1988. At this conference God opened me up to God's work and the ministry of the Holy Spirit in new ways. Following this conference I experienced renewal in my personal walk with the Lord and renewed energy in my pastoral ministry. Along with that renewal came a time of personal struggle and congregational suffering. I discovered that walking with the Spirit is not always an easy or painless road but that God is with us on it.

Third, I wish to acknowledge some of the individuals who helped make this book possible. I thank my advisor and friend, Dr. Manuel Ortiz, who mentored me through my doctoral program and the writing of this material as a course. I am grateful for his love, insights, direction, encouragement, and advice. I thank Peter and Donna Dykstra for their use of "the cabin" on the Delaware as a place of writing, reflection, and rewriting. I also thank Waldron Scott for his keen and insightful criticism, his questions, his challenges, and his invaluable assistance with the current revision. I thank my best friend and colleague in ministry, Rev. Stafford Miller, with whom "iron sharpens iron," for helping me to continue to grow in the work and power of the Holy Spirit and for encouraging me to publish this material. Finally, to all my colleagues in ministry—and especially to the pastors of the Paterson Pastor's Workshop, who have accepted me and allowed me to learn from their wisdom and African American experience—I am deeply indebted.

Fourth, I want to thank my family. I thank my parents for teaching me from an early age by their example and life what it meant to believe in and follow Jesus. I thank my son Benjamin for his encouraging love for me and for his patience with me when I was too preoccupied with ministry. I thank especially my wife, Debra Joy, for her selfless love and inspiration, her faithful support and encouragement, her keen insights and questions, and her constant testing and prodding. Through our hours of debates and discussion the truths of Scripture became more clear and concise. Through her hours of reading and correcting draft manuscripts, I was given the opportunity to clarify what I was trying to say.

Finally, I thank God, my Father; Jesus Christ, my Lord and Savior; and the Holy Spirit, my counselor and comforter. Truly I have learned as much about myself as I have about God.

—John A. Algera

Contents

INTRODUCTION

The power and work of an almighty god has captured the interest and imagination of people for centuries. Every culture and religion cherishes stories of how its gods performed miracles and displayed power. In the Old Testament, Yahweh reveals himself as the one true God over all others. In the New Testament, Jesus, as the only begotten Son of God, reveals God through proclamation and demonstration. He commissions his disciples to do the same and pours out his Holy Spirit on all true believers.

Throughout church history, people have experienced, witnessed, and documented miracles. During the eighteenth and nineteenth centuries, miracles were frequently evident in the great revivals in England and the United States. In the last 100 years of church history, the Pentecostal movement has highlighted the miraculous and supernatural work of God and the power of the Holy Spirit. In the late 1960s and early 1970s, the Charismatic or Neo-Pentecostal movement continued this emphasis and influenced many mainline denominations. In the 1980s the Pentecostal/Charismatic renewal began to have a dramatic impact on world evangelization and the growth of the church.

The so-called "third wave" that began in the 1980s is similar to and yet distinct from the Pentecostal/Charismatic movement of the '60s and '70s. This "third wave" is characterized by

- ▸ spiritual renewal
- ▸ use of all spiritual gifts
- ▸ signs and wonders
- ▸ healing
- ▸ power encounters
- ▸ deliverance
- ▸ spiritual warfare

It has its theological foundations in the power of the Holy Spirit and in the presence of the kingdom of God and rule of Christ here and now.

The Pentecostal/Charismatic renewal in the Holy Spirit now sweeping across the globe has important lessons to teach my own denomination and others of the Reformed stream. Because of growing interest in this movement and because of some expressed concerns, Synod 2004 of the Christian Reformed Church appointed a study committee to examine the biblical teaching, Reformed confessions, theological implications, and pastoral dimensions related to third wave Pentecostalism (spiritual warfare, deliverance ministries, and so forth) with a view to providing advice to the churches.

— *Acts of Synod 2004*, pp. 608-609.

Denominational leaders are coming to a growing realization that in order for the church to be an effective witness in today's world it must be open to the work of God in new ways. For the last 20 years, Reformed missionaries and pastors engaged on the front lines of ministry have been calling the church to see what God can do. I'll share three examples from leaders within the Christian Reformed Church.

In 1984 pastor and author Donald J. Griffioen concluded a chapter on spiritual gifts with this summary of the need for the power of the Holy Spirit in ministry: . . . I am suggesting that a spirit of renewal in the church should keep us open to new, unexpected, and surprise workings of God in our day that do not rule out the possibility of miracles. God wants his church today equipped with the same power of the Holy Spirit and variety of spiritual gifts experienced in the early church. We must be open to these gifts in the church today, for not to do so is to resist the Spirit of God.

—*Open Windows and Open Doors* (Christian Reformed Board of Evangelism of Greater Grand Rapids, 1984), p. 132.

In 1988 I attended a conference sponsored by Christian Reformed Home Missions called "Kingdom Power and Evangelism." This conference was held to explore the vital need for the power of the Holy Spirit in carrying out the evangelistic ministry of the church. In one keynote address, Dr. Gene Rubingh, former missionary and missionary executive, challenged us with the need for proclamation *and* demonstration of God's power in evangelism:

I maintain that our laudable balance on the issue of the scope of salvation is not complemented by a balance on our view of the demonstrations of salvation. We have worked almost exclusively with program evangelism, with structures, projects, timelines, budgets, and reports and omitted the immediate, the existential, and the confrontational. It is out of our orbit. We have engaged in a battle of the intellect, but the world is not asking,

"What does your God know?" The world is asking, "What does your God do?"
— "*Kingdom and Power in Scripture and Theology*," (Church Development Resources, Christian Reformed Home Missions, 1988).

Although the historic Reformed Creeds, including the well-loved Question and Answer 1 of the Heidelberg Catechism, speak boldly of how Christ has "set me free from the tyranny of the devil," many in our Reformed circles are unequipped to fully experience that freedom. Several years ago at a training event held by our classis (a regional group of churches), we invited pastor and author Jeff Stam to speak on spiritual warfare. In the introduction to his book, Stam explains why there is a need—especially in Reformed circles—for yet one more book on the subject of spiritual warfare:

> . . . mainly because my Reformed tradition hasn't done much with this topic. That's not because people in our churches are not affected or interested (we have addressed some related topics). I'm convinced our neglect is due to our need to tie up all the theological "loose ends." Perhaps we need to remind ourselves that dealing with the reality of Satan and his powers was so central in Reformation thinking that it became the major theme of the Reformation's "fight" song ("A Mighty Fortress Is Our God").
> —*Straight Talk About Spiritual Warfare*, CRC Publications, 1999.

I mention these examples because I have noticed a large gap between belief and practice in Reformed thinking. We have a rich heritage of biblical teaching and Reformed theology, but we have impeded our ministry by failing to apply that theology. Our theology of the kingdom of God has found expression in many kingdom ministries, yet we've missed aspects of kingdom power. Our theology of the Holy Spirit has stressed holy living, yet we've missed the full use and outpouring of all the gifts of the Spirit and the power of the Spirit. Although we pray for healing for those who are sick, we don't usually expect that God will miraculously heal them. Although we believe Satan exists, we have little consciousness of his daily personal attacks. Although we believe in the Holy Spirit, we have not been taught what it means to be "filled with the Spirit."

The challenge facing my own denomination and others of the Reformed tradition is to combine the richness of our Reformed understanding of Scripture and Christianity with a new awareness of the power of God available to us today. Recognition of the lordship of Christ, the presence of the kingdom of God, and the power of the Holy Spirit are vital ingredients for the growth of the church in the world today. This recognition finds expression in the use of all the gifts of the Holy Spirit and is demonstrated in the fruits of the Spirit. It is manifested in signs, wonders, and miracles today. It has implications both personally and congregationally for prayer, worship, word and deed evangelism, discipleship, and fellowship. It also has implications for social, political, and economic structures. It is evidenced in the "healing" and "exorcisms" of both personal and structural "ills."

In a recent Bible study on the book of Acts, our class observed that the proclamation of the gospel was accompanied by signs and wonders that resulted in the growth of the church. These signs and wonders included

▶ healing of illness and disease.
▶ casting out of demons.
▶ mass conversions.
▶ deliverance from prison.
▶ speaking in other languages.
▶ other extraordinary events.

During our study one class member asked, "Why doesn't God still do such signs and wonders today?" That question has become the foundation for this book.

It is my prayer that this book will help you, through personal study or as a member of a small group, to

▶ gain a biblical understanding of the presence of the kingdom of God and the lordship of Christ.
▶ develop an openness to the power of the Holy Spirit, to the use of all the gifts of the Holy Spirit, and to continual filling by the Spirit.
▶ increase awareness of the ongoing battle still fought on earth between the kingdom of God and the kingdom of Satan.
▶ develop an openness to the experience and practice of signs and wonders at personal, congregational, and societal levels.
▶ more readily recognize and celebrate signs and wonders that God is already doing.
▶ appreciate how signs and wonders fit into a Reformed worldview and way of worship and witness.

Each of the twelve chapters of this book include

▸ words from other sources that help set the stage for the section's topic.
▸ a brief introduction to each section's topic.
▸ an in-depth look at each topic.
▸ testimonies from people who have witnessed the power of the Holy Spirit in all ages.
▸ "Reformed Reflections" with passages from one or more of the Reformed creeds and confessions and a suggested thought for personal or group reflection.
▸ suggestions for prayer and practice to stimulate spiritual growth and discipleship.

Each section concludes with a list of suggested references for further reading and study.

One of my favorite hymns when I was growing up and one I still love to sing is "Praise to the Lord, the Almighty." The third stanza concludes with this line: "Ponder anew, what the Almighty can do, as with his love he befriends you" (Joachim Neander, 1680; tr. Catherine Winkworth, 1863, alt.). This book is an attempt to do just that—to ponder anew what the Almighty can do. May you be blessed as you too ponder anew!

—John Algera

CHAPTER ONE

BIBLICAL TEACHINGS
ON SIGNS AND WONDERS

AND MOSES LIFTED UP HIS ROD OVER THE RED SEA; AND GOD WITH
A BLAST OF HIS NOSTRILS BLEW THE WATERS APART. AND THE
WAVES ROLLED BACK AND STOOD UP IN A PILE, AND LEFT A PATH
THROUGH THE MIDDLE OF THE SEA DRY AS THE SANDS OF THE
DESERT. AND THE CHILDREN OF ISRAEL ALL CROSSED OVER ON TO
THE OTHER SIDE. WHEN PHARAOH SAW THEM CROSSING DRY, HE
DASHED ON IN BEHIND THEM—OLD PHARAOH GOT ABOUT HALF WAY
CROSS, AND GOD UNLASHED THE WATERS, AND THE WAVES RUSHED
BACK TOGETHER, AND PHARAOH AND ALL HIS ARMY GOT LOST, AND
ALL HIS HOST GOT DROWNED. AND MOSES SANG AND MIRIAM
DANCED, AND THE PEOPLE SHOUTED FOR JOY, AND GOD LED THE
HEBREW CHILDREN ON TILL THEY REACHED THE PROMISED LAND.
LISTEN!—LISTEN! ALL YOU SONS OF PHARAOH. WHO DO YOU THINK
CAN HOLD GOD'S PEOPLE WHEN THE LORD GOD HIMSELF HAS SAID,
LET MY PEOPLE GO?

—James Weldon Johnson, "Let My People Go," *God's Trombones*,
Penguin Books, 1927, p. 52. © 1927, Viking Press, Inc.; renewed © 1955,
Grace Nail Johnson. Used by permission of Viking Penguin,
a division of Penguin Group (USA), Inc.

O ne day a cardinal was showing off St. Peter's basilica in Rome to a visiting country priest. Pointing to the beautiful buildings around the huge courtyard, the cardinal boasted: "No longer do we have to say like Peter said at the temple, 'Silver and gold have I none.'" "Yes, that's true," observed the priest, "but neither can we say, 'Take up your bed and walk.'"

Unfortunately the same has become true in many churches.

Some of the Bible stories I remember best from Sunday school were of the healings performed by Jesus and the disciples. I can still remember making a house out of a shoebox, cutting a hole in the roof, and lowering down a cardboard man on a cardboard stretcher suspended from four strings. We learned about the faith of the man's four friends and that Jesus made him walk. But as I recall this and other Bible stories, I realize that as I grew up I was unintentionally taught that such miracles occurred during Bible times only—not today.

I recently reread the Bible. My goal was to observe the place of signs, wonders, and miracles in the life of God's people and in the growth of the early church. It was a wonderful experience. I saw how free God is to accomplish his purposes in ordinary *and* extraordinary ways.

This chapter will explore the idea of "signs and wonders" in depth. We'll look at exactly what they are and how they were understood by the biblical writers and those who experienced them. We will

▸ review some of the miracles of the Old and New Testament.
▸ study the Greek and Hebrew words used to describe signs, wonders, and miracles in the Bible.
▸ reflect on the theological and historical uses of these words.

OVERVIEW OF
MIRACLES IN THE BIBLE

PHYSICAL HEALINGS
The Old Testament provides many references to miraculous healing of physical illness, including the healing of

▸ Miriam, who was struck with leprosy when she and Aaron opposed Moses (Num. 12:10-15).

- the Israelites, who were bitten by snakes after complaining against God and Moses (Num. 21:9).
- Naaman, who also suffered from leprosy (2 Kings 5).
- Hezekiah, who at the point of death was given an extra fifteen years of life (2 Kings 20).

The New Testament gospels are full of references to people healed by Jesus. In Matthew 4:23 we read, "Jesus went throughout Galilee, teaching in their synagogues, preaching the good news of the kingdom, and healing every disease and sickness among the people." When questioned by John the Baptist if he was the Messiah, Jesus answered, "Go back and report to John what you hear and see: The blind receive sight, the lame walk, those who have leprosy are cured, the deaf hear, the dead are raised, and the good news is preached to the poor" (Matt. 11:4-5).

But these acts weren't only for Jesus to do. Jesus commissioned his disciples to "heal the sick" (Luke 10:9)—a task they continued after Jesus' ascension. In Acts, Luke (who was himself a physician) records numerous physical healings, including those done by

- Peter, who healed "a man crippled from birth" (Acts 3:1-10).
- Stephen, who "did great wonders and miraculous signs" (6:8).
- Philip, who did "miraculous signs. . . . evil spirits came out of many, and many paralytics and cripples were healed" (8:6-7).
- Ananias, who placed his hands on Saul, and "immediately, something like scales fell from Saul's eyes, and he could see again" (9:10-19).
- Paul and Barnabas, who were enabled by God's grace to "do miraculous signs and wonders" (14:3).
- Paul, who healed "a man crippled in his feet, who was lame from birth and had never walked" (14:8-10).

RESURRECTIONS
In the Old and New Testament we also read of people being raised from the dead. Consider these specific examples:

- Elijah raised the widow of Zarephath's son (1 Kings 17).
- Elisha raised the Shunammite woman's son (2 Kings 4).
- Jesus raised Jairus's daughter (Matt. 9:18-25), the widow of Nain's son (Luke 7:11-17), and his friend Lazarus (John 11:1-44).
- Peter raised Dorcas (Acts 9:40).
- Paul raised Eutychus (Acts 20:10).

Jesus' own resurrection is recorded in detail by all four gospel writers. Matthew also notes that many of the dead saints of Jerusalem were raised on Good Friday and walked around the city after Jesus himself arose (Matt. 27:53).

POWER CONFRONTATIONS WITH ENEMIES OR SATAN

Another type of miracle we see in Scripture involves dramatic power confrontations between

▸ Yahweh and false gods.
▸ God's people and heathen people.
▸ Jesus and his disciples versus the devil and his demons.

In the Old Testament, Jericho's walls fell after the Israelites marched around the city for seven days (Josh. 6). The Philistine god Dagon fell down before the ark of the covenant (1 Sam. 5). Elijah called down fire from heaven to defeat the prophets of Baal at Mount Carmel (1 Kings 18).

In the New Testament, Jesus' ministry includes defeating Satan and casting out demons. More than thirty references in Matthew, Mark, and Luke refer to Jesus' ministry of exorcism. Jesus also commissioned his disciples and gave them authority "to overcome all the power of the enemy" (Luke 10:19). At his ascension Jesus gave them authority over Satan and his hosts (Mark 16:17; Matt. 28:18). In Acts, the apostles cast out demons and evil spirits (5:16; 8:7; 19:12).

MIRACLES IN NATURE

Scripture provides us with many examples of miracles accomplished by extraordinary events in nature. In the Old Testament, God used nature in extraordinary ways to

▸ destroy humankind and save Noah, his family, and the animals in the ark when "all the springs of the great deep burst forth, and the floodgates of the heavens were opened" (Gen. 7:11-12).
▸ destroy Sodom and Gomorrah by fire (Gen. 19).
▸ cause Pharaoh to let the Israelites go after the ten plagues came upon Egypt (Ex. 7-11).
▸ deliver Moses and the Israelites through the parting of the Red Sea (Ex. 13) and the Jordan River (Joshua 3).
▸ provide for his people by sending manna, quail, and water in the wilderness (Ex. 16-17).

- give victory to Joshua when the sun stood still for a full day (Josh. 10).
- feed Elijah when ravens brought him bread and meat morning and night (1 Kings 17).
- protect Daniel by closing the lions' mouths (Dan. 6).
- shelter Jonah from the heat by causing a vine to grow up over him (Jonah 4).

In the New Testament, miracles in nature were a part of Jesus' life, beginning with his birth to a virgin (Luke 2). During his ministry, Jesus

- turned water into wine (John 2:6-10).
- stilled a storm (Mark 4:35-41).
- walked on water and invited Peter to come to him (Matt. 14:25-29).
- multiplied a boy's bread and fish to feed 5,000 people (John 6).
- caused a fig tree to wither (Mark 11:21).
- filled empty nets with fish (John 21:6).

During the last three hours of Jesus' suffering on the cross, a deep darkness came over all the land, and the earth shook at the moment of his death (Matt. 27:45-51). After his resurrection, Jesus was able to appear and disappear instantly (Luke, 24:31, 36) and pass through doors (John 20:26).

Miracles in nature continued after Jesus' ascension. Paul and Silas were released from prison by a violent earthquake (Acts 16:26), and Philip was transported to another place by the Spirit (Acts 8:39).

WORD STUDY: SIGNS, WONDERS, MIRACLES, MIGHTY WORKS

The Bible uses several different words in the Old Testament Hebrew and New Testament Greek to describe what we call miracles. These words include *signs, wonders, miracles,* and *mighty works.* Let's briefly review the biblical usage of each and note how they are sometimes used together.

SIGNS

The word *sign* or *signs* is used by itself to refer to a distinguishing mark or indication, as in these two passages:

- "This will be a sign to you: You will find a baby wrapped in cloths and lying in a manger" (Luke 2:12).
- "You know how to interpret the appearance of the sky, but you cannot interpret the signs of the times" (Matt. 16:3).

This term may also refer to something that is unusual and different from nature. In this use the word is translated as *sign, miraculous sign,* or *miracle* depending on the context and translation. When Jesus changes water to wine, this is called "the first of his miraculous signs" (John 2:11). The Pharisees ask Jesus for a "miraculous sign" to demonstrate his authority (Matt. 12:38).

In most New Testament references, signs are performed by God himself, by Jesus Christ, or by the people of God. But the term can also refer to a miracle performed by Satan, demons, or people serving him. Jesus warns of this: "For false Christs and false prophets will appear and perform great signs and miracles to deceive even the elect—if that were possible" (Matt. 24:24).

The word *sign* is used in the Old Testament to denote something that can be visibly seen to demonstrate God's power or care. David pleads, "Give me a sign of your goodness" (Ps. 86:17). A sign always points beyond itself to someone or something else.

WONDERS

A *wonder* is an awe-inspiring or terrifying act that manifests supernatural power. The word *wonder* in the Old Testament refers to a "special display of God's power" or "token of future event" (Brown, Francis; S.R. Driver; and Charles A. Briggs, *A Hebrew and English Lexicon of the Old Testament,* Clarendon Press, 1907, pp. 68-69).

God is always behind a wonder, and God does wonders as part of his rule and reign. "Remember the wonders he has done, his miracles and the judgments he pronounced" (1 Chron. 16:12). The word itself describes the human reaction to God's act—wonder!

SIGNS AND WONDERS

In the translation of the Old Testament Hebrew into Greek, the phrase *signs and wonders* refers primarily to the plagues God brought upon Egypt to deliver Israel. "Before our eyes the LORD sent miraculous signs and wonders—great and terrible—upon Egypt and Pharaoh" (Deut. 6:23).

In the New Testament Greek, the word *teras* ("wonders") is used only together with the word *semeion* ("signs"). *Signs and wonders* is a technical term used in Greek to refer to miracles done by

▸ Jesus (John 4:48; Acts 2:22).
▸ the disciples and apostles (Acts 4:30; 5:12; 6:8; 7:36; 14:3; Rom. 15:19; 2 Cor. 12:12; Heb. 2:4).
▸ Satan or his agents (Matt. 24:24; Mark 13:22; 2 Thess. 2:9).

Whether performed by Jesus or Satan, signs and wonders always relate to an extraordinary event that calls for our attention.

In three passages, the word *power* (*dunamis*) is added to *signs and wonders* and translated as "miracles." In one reference, *power* is substituted for *wonders* to make the phrase *signs and miracles* (Acts 8:13).

MIRACLES

Biblical words that are translated as "miracles" often have to do with God's power and strength. *Power* (Ex. 15:6; Ps. 77:14) and *strength* (Ps. 46:1; 84:7) carry a unique emphasis in the Old Testament. They refer to a personal God who uses his power to care for his people. The exodus event was a unique example of the power of God to deliver his people (Ex. 12:31-51).

This sense of power is carried over into the New Testament in the use of *dunamis* in Greek. This word is defined as "the outward expression of power; deed of power, miracle, wonder" (Bauer, Walter, *A Greek-English Lexicon of the New Testament,* University of Chicago Press, 1957, p. 207). It is

▸ used with *signs and wonders* occasionally (2 Thess. 2:9; Acts 2:22; 2 Cor. 12:12
▸ simply translated as *miracle* (Heb. 2:4).
▸ used independently (Matt. 7:22; 11:20, 23; 13:54, 58; Luke 10:13; 19:37; 1 Cor. 12:10, 28).

Another Greek word for power is *exousia*. This word is never translated as "miracle" and is used to describe the distinct power of God the Father, Son, and Holy Spirit and how that power is given to God's people.

MIGHTY WORKS

The final Greek word used to refer to miracles is *ergon*. In the translation of the Old Testament into Greek, this word is used to translate various Hebrew words that refer to the mighty works or miracles of God. "For what god is there in heaven or on earth who can do the deeds and mighty works you do?" (Deut. 3:24).

In the New Testament, *ergon* refers to the deeds of God and Jesus. The gospel writer John especially likes to use this term, and it is translated "miracle" in the NIV in John 7:3, 21; 10:25, 38; 14:11; 15:24.

WORD STUDY SUMMARY

On the basis of this word study, we can say that the Bible speaks of signs, wonders, miracles, and mighty works as observable manifestations of God's power. In biblical times, these manifestations took many forms and could not always be explained by the laws of nature or human reason; yet neither did they necessarily contradict these laws. Generally, they accompany the proclamation of the Word of God or the establishment of the rule of God. They can include something as spectacular as the parting of the Red Sea or something as small as one person's healing. Counterfeit signs and miracles can also be from Satan. Specifically, we can conclude that

▸ a sign was always an event that pointed to something beyond itself.
▸ a wonder was always an event that was awe-inspiring, causing observers to wonder.
▸ a miracle was an event outside of normal human experience, something extraordinary.

HISTORICAL AND THEOLOGICAL REFLECTIONS

Establishing what a miracle was in Bible times does not necessarily tell us what a miracle is today. *Webster's New Collegiate Dictionary* defines the word *miracle* as "an extraordinary event manifesting divine intervention in human affairs . . . an extremely outstanding or unusual event, thing, or accomplishment." Because such a definition is open to subjective interpretation, people take several different positions on what defines a miracle.

One position recognizes an event as a miracle only if scientific evidence confirms that the laws of nature or human reason can't explain it. A second position sees miracles as part of God's revelation before the canon of Scripture was closed. This position states that miracles ended with the age of the apostles and today God's providence is the evidence of God's ongoing work and power. A third position denies the existence of miracles at any time, believing that God only works through naturally created channels. A fourth position holds that the miraculous is based on subjective experience, not on scientific evidence. A brief historical review will explain each of these positions.

THE EARLY CHURCH

In the early centuries of the Christian church, miracles were recorded and recounted. They involved physical and mental healings, exorcisms, unexplained food supplied to the poor, and extraordinary conversions. Saint Augustine lists many in his classic work *The City of God,* written in A.D. 425. Often these miracles were closely related to the relics of martyrs and sacred places or images. Miracles were considered "extraordinary" works of God that defied the laws of nature or other explanation. This position is still evident in the lengthy Roman Catholic process of confirming and authenticating a miracle.

THE REFORMATION

A different position on miracles arose at the time of the Reformation. In reaction to Roman Catholic "supernaturalism," John Calvin and the Reformers taught that the miracles and supernatural gifts of the Holy Spirit only accompanied the initial presentation of the gospel and ended with the apostles. They believed that the miracles of the Scriptures were real and that God could still do miracles. But since God now revealed himself through the Word, God chose not to reveal himself in other supernatural ways. In Reformation thinking, miracles were specific, supernatural, and extraordinary works of God, but they were isolated to the age of the apostles, so no verification or confirmation was needed.

THE ENLIGHTENMENT

A denial of miracles arose out of the seventeenth century enlightenment and a scientific approach to theology and the Bible. It sought to explain miraculous events through scientific evidence or to deny them completely.

This position appears in much liberal Christianity and in attempts to prove the truth of the Bible through scientific inquiry alone.

THE PENTECOSTAL MOVEMENT

A fourth position arose out of a synthesis of the first two positions. Movements arising out of the Reformation, and later revivals leading up to and including the Pentecostal movement, combined elements of both of these views. Every aspect of God's providence that contradicted the laws of nature or was not readily explainable was labeled a miracle. This could include the end of a toothache, the finding of a parking spot, the healing of cancer, or deliverance from demons. Confirmation of miracles was no longer required by "the Church," but was based on individual subjective judgment that included all aspects of God's providence.

TOWARD A WORKING DEFINITION

None of the above four positions satisfactorily answers the question of whether there are miracles today. According to our word study, the Bible refers to miracles as the intervention of God in the lives of people in new, surprising, and extraordinary ways. Signs are events that point to something beyond themselves. Wonders leave people awe-struck by the power of God. These occurrences may or may not violate the laws of nature and may or may not be scientifically verifiable.

Theologian Vern Poythress warns of the dangers of definitions with "fuzzy boundaries" and offers a brief working definition that stresses more the purpose than the character of a miracle. "A miracle is an extraordinary visible act of God to deliver his people and attest his word" (Poythress, Vern S., *Symphonic Theology*, Academia Books, 1987, p. 105). Although Poythress believes that miracles have ceased because special revelation is complete, he still recognizes mighty acts of God in our day, though he does not call them miracles.

On the other hand, anthropologist Charles Kraft recognizes the ordinary and extraordinary power of God in defining miracles as normal events in the kingdom of God. He says:

> What we call "miracles" then, are expected by Jesus to be normal occurrences in our part of the kingdom, as in all other parts. They are not, as we have been taught, to be regarded

as interferences by God in a domain from which he ordinarily keeps his distance.

—*Christianity with Power,* Servant Publications, p. 115.

Kraft appeals for a removal of the term *miracle* from the realm of the extraordinary. He sees miracles as a normal expectation within the kingdom of God along with salvation, obedience, healing, deliverance, and every other aspect of Christian service and love. This emphasis recognizes that miracles and signs and wonders are "extraordinary" events that happen in the ordinary routines of life.

Dr. Lewis B. Smedes, in a study for Fuller Theological Seminary, warns of the danger of preoccupation with miracles and the distorted belief that God is only present when something spectacular is being done.

> In the Biblical view, a miracle is a signal that God is, for a moment and for a special purpose, walking down paths he does not usually walk. A miracle is not a sign that a God who is usually absent is, for the moment, present. It is only a sign that God who is always present in creative power is working here and now in an unfamiliar style.
>
> —*Ministry and the Miraculous,*
> Fuller Theological Seminary, 1987, pp. 48-49.

We can conclude that miracles and signs and wonders that are of God will always point to God. Also, we must recognize that although God's miracles are always at God's discretion, God also responds to his peoples' requests. Biblically, God's mighty acts are not bound to scientific confirmation but to faith testimony. Also, in their biblical use these terms do not refer to every aspect of the grace or providence of God but to extraordinary evidences of that providence. Although God is at work in every aspect of our lives, not every aspect of his providence in our lives is considered miraculous. Although miracles may be *ordinary* for God, their occurrence is always *extraordinary* for people.

An evidence of the Reformed emphasis on the sovereignty of God is that we cry out to God for such miracles, and we put our faith in God's response. When defining such miracles, we may not be able to avoid fuzzy boundaries. A miracle may come with or without medical technology. A miracle may be subjectively experienced by only one person. But when God does a miracle, people know it and testify to it.

For our working definition, we will consider signs, wonders, miracles, and mighty works of God to be exceptional, extraordinary moves of God that

- reveal God's power and glory.
- change situations and circumstances.
- cause people to wonder—to sit up and take notice.
- demonstrate the Word of God and the presence of the kingdom of God.

As God says, "Behold, I am making a covenant with you. Before all your people I will do wonders never before done in any nation in all the world. The people you live among will see how awesome is the work that I, the LORD, will do for you (Ex. 34:10).

TESTIMONIES FROM . . .

SAINT AUGUSTINE (A.D. 426)

Even now, therefore, many miracles are wrought, the same God who wrought those we read of is still performing them, by whom He will and as He will. . . . There were seven brothers and three sisters of a noble family of the Cappadocian Caesarea . . . all of them were seized with a hideous shaking in all their limbs. Two of them came to Hippo. . . . Easter arrived, and on the Lord's day, in the morning, when there was now a large crowd present, and the young man was holding the bars of the holy place where the relics were, and praying, suddenly he fell down, and lay precisely as if asleep, but not trembling as he was wont to do even in sleep. All present were astonished. Some were alarmed, some were moved with pity; and while some were for lifting him up, others prevented them, and said they should rather wait and see what would result. And behold! he rose up, and trembled no more, for he was healed, and stood quite well, scanning those who were scanning him. Who then refrained himself from praising God? . . . the church was full, and ringing with the shouts of joy. "Thanks to God! Praised be God!"

—The City of God, translated by Marcus Dods,
Random House, 1950, p. 830.

REV. CHARLES UKEN (1992)

Umbanda is a modern, urban, Brazilian religion that is growing in both numbers of adherents and influence. It is a syncretistic religious stream in Brazil and touches the lives of people in every social class. . . . The most important point of contact is the point of need. Can the Christian pray for deliverance for the sick, the oppressed and the unemployed? Can he or she expel a demon in the name of Christ? Does the Christian have faith to expect the intervention and action of God? Signs, wonders, and God's miraculous power speak to the Umbandist's heart where charity, medicine, or financial assistance leave him cold.

—"Spiritism and the Brazilian City,"
Urban Mission, May, 1992, pp. 20, 31.

REFORMED REFLECTIONS

THE HEIDELBERG CATECHISM, Q&A 26

**Q. What do you believe when you say,
"I believe in God, the Father Almighty, creator
of heaven and earth"?**

A. That the eternal Father of our Lord Jesus Christ,
who out of nothing created heaven and earth
and everything in them,
who still upholds and rules them
by his eternal counsel and providence,
is my God and Father
because of Christ his Son.

I trust him so much that I do not doubt
he will provide
whatever I need
for body and soul,
and he will turn to my good
whatever adversity he sends me
in this sad world.

He is able to do this because he is almighty God;
He desires to do this because he is a faithful Father.

Reflect on the relationship between the providence of
God and the miracles of God.

QUESTIONS TO THINK ABOUT

▸ On the basis of the biblical teachings we've discussed and of our word
study, do you believe that God still does signs, wonders, and miracles? Why or why not?

▸ According to Scripture, do miracles have to be "unusual" or "extraordinary" experiences? Explain.

▸ How would you respond to someone who says that a miracle must be
scientifically verifiable?

- Briefly describe a miracle that you have experienced personally or heard about.
- What are some dangers in the miraculous?
- 1 Corinthians 12:28 refers to "workers of miracles" as being part of the body of Christ. Who are the "workers of miracles" today?

PRAYER AND PRACTICE

Pray aloud the first part of the song Moses and the Israelites sang after crossing the Red Sea:

> "I WILL SING TO THE LORD,
> FOR HE IS HIGHLY EXALTED.
> THE HORSE AND ITS RIDER
> HE HAS HURLED INTO THE SEA.
> THE LORD IS MY STRENGTH AND MY SONG;
> HE HAS BECOME MY SALVATION.
> HE IS MY GOD, AND I WILL PRAISE HIM,
> MY FATHER'S GOD, AND I WILL EXALT HIM."
> —EXODUS 15:1-2

Praise God right now for ways you have experienced God's strength and salvation in your life.

ADDITIONAL RESOURCES

BOOKS
- Gundry, Stanley N., ed. *Are Miraculous Gifts for Today? 4 Views.* Richard B. Gaffin, Jr.; Robert L. Saucy; C. Samuel Storms; Douglas A. Oss. Grand Rapids, Mich.: Zondervan, 1996.
- McClung, Grant. "Pentecostals: The Sequel." *Christianity Today*, April 2006.
- Trammel, Madison and Rob Moll. "Grading the Movement: Three Leaders Talk Frankly About Pentecostalism." *Christianity Today*, April 2006.
- Wagner, C. Peter. *The Third Wave of the Holy Spirit.* Ann Arbor: Servant Publications, 1988.

CHAPTER TWO

WHAT'S YOUR WORLDVIEW?

DIDN'T MY LORD DELIVER DANIEL,
DELIVER DANIEL, DELIVER DANIEL?
DIDN'T MY LORD DELIVER DANIEL,
AND WHY NOT-A EVERY MAN?
HE DELIVERED DANIEL FROM THE LIONS' DEN,
JONAH FROM THE BELLY OF THE WHALE,
AND THE HEBREW CHILDREN FROM THE FIERY FURNACE,
AND WHY NOT EVERY MAN?

—Traditional

I recently posted a large map of the world in my office. Nearly every person who saw it made the same comment: "That map is upside down!"

I had intentionally put the South Pole on top. Why, I wondered, do we consider the world "right side up" when North America and Europe are on top? What is the correct view of the world?

How people view the world and perceive reality varies greatly and is influenced by race, culture, education, upbringing and expectations. This became very clear to me several years ago. After a fall, I was diagnosed with a broken knee and torn cartilage that demanded immediate arthroscopic surgery. Pre-admission tests were run, the operating room scheduled, and personal and congregational prayers offered. But as I lay on the operating table with an intravenous tube in my arm and with the anesthesiologist ready to put me under, the doctor reexamined my leg. Although the knee was still broken, full movement was restored and surgery was no longer needed.

Was this a miracle of God? A misdiagnosis by the doctor? An unexplained readjustment of the cartilage? I jokingly suggested to the doctor that the Lord had beat him to the cure, but more serious questions and possibilities ran around in my own mind. Why was it so hard for me to accept this as a miraculous healing from the Lord? Why did I need a logical, physiological, medical, and scientific explanation for what took place? As a pastor, I believed in miracles, regularly prayed for peoples' healing, and had even introduced a healing emphasis in my congregation. Yet I struggled to unquestioningly accept a healing in my own life.

My personal struggle illustrates how much my worldview affects my understanding of God's power and work. This section will help you examine your own worldview as we

▶ define what a worldview is.
▶ look at several worldviews that influence us today.
▶ define a biblical worldview.
▶ examine the impact of various worldviews on our view of signs and wonders, on ministry and missions, and on our Reformed perspective.

What Is a Worldview?

Theologian Timothy Warner gives a helpful working definition for understanding the term *worldview:*

> Worldview is the thought system we develop for explaining the world around us and our experiences in it. It is determined almost entirely by the society in which we grow up. In most instances, it is something we absorb subconsciously more than something we adopt after careful study, although study can change worldview drastically.
>
> —*Spiritual Warfare,* Crossway Books, 1991, p. 24.

In his excellent study *The Universe Next Door* (InterVarsity Press, 1988, pp. 17-18), James Sire lists a series of questions, the answers to which tell us a lot about a person's worldview:

- ▸ What is prime reality—the "really real"?
- ▸ What is the nature of external reality—that is, the world around us?
- ▸ What is a human being?
- ▸ What happens to a person at death?
- ▸ Why is it possible to know anything at all?
- ▸ How do we know what is right and wrong?
- ▸ What is the meaning of human history?

Influential Worldviews

Let's look briefly at five prominent worldviews that impact people today:

- ▸ theism
- ▸ deism
- ▸ animism
- ▸ the New Age movement
- ▸ postmodernism

THEISM

Theism is a belief in one god. Likewise, polytheism is a belief in many gods. The Israelites were commanded by Yahweh to be theists—to *"have no other gods before me"* (Ex. 20:3). Today's versions of Judaism and

Islam are also examples of theism. Christian theism is summarized in statements of faith such as the Apostles' Creed. This creed proclaims a personal God involved in the day-to-day lives of people, who, even though fallen into sin, are restored in their relationship to God through Jesus. Due to the rapid spread of Christianity after the ascension of Christ, theism quickly became the predominant worldview of the Western world.

DEISM
Deism is the belief in a transcendent god who created the world but then left it to its own fate. The image of God winding up a clock and then letting it run its course is often used to describe this worldview. Although deism has existed in various forms throughout history, its current influence in America arose out of the French enlightenment. It has had a tremendous effect in the Western world, especially in America, by portraying a distant and impersonal God.

ANIMISM
Animism is the belief that everything in the world (rocks, trees, houses) is inhabited (or "animated" by spirits. Animists can be found in Africa, Asia, South and Central America, and is illustrated in the religion of Native Americans and First Nations peoples in North America. An acute sense of the spirit realm and its involvement in daily life is evident in this worldview.

NEW AGE MOVEMENT
The New Age movement has close ties to naturalism, pantheism, animism, and Eastern mysticism. This worldview stresses pursuing a "higher consciousness" and achieving harmony with nature and the spirit realm. Followers desire to accept all viewpoints as having equal claim to the truth. A new emphasis on spirituality in all forms is in fashion. Many "supernatural events" similar to miracles and signs and wonders take place among people holding to this worldview.

POSTMODERNISM
Postmodernism, which is embraced in North America, is a reaction to Western scientific enlightenment. It is characterized by a rejection of the enlightenment hope in human progress and is deeply pessimistic about the human condition.

This worldview finds truth to be relative to one's situation and place in life. According to postmodernists, no one can claim to have or know absolute truth or absolute right or wrong; each person should do what is right in his or her own eyes. No common beliefs or foundations related to God or people exist.

DEFINING A BIBLICAL/REFORMED WORLDVIEW

Defining a biblical worldview is not as easy as it seems. The Bible encompasses over two thousand years of history, during which its authors' views of the world were constantly changing. In the ancient Middle-Eastern world, other gods were acknowledged and worshiped along with Yahweh (Gen. 31:19) until God strictly forbade this practice in the Ten Commandments (Ex. 20:3).

The Old Covenant and the New Covenant views of the world vary widely. This contrast of worldviews is also evident in the different ways today's Christians interpret Scripture and understand how God works. Since the scientific revolution in the seventeenth century, the Western Christian worldview has changed rapidly. Under its influence, a growing secularization of Christianity challenges the authority of Scripture and the power of God.

What is commonly understood as a Reformed world-and-life view is described in terms of the biblical accounts of

▶ creation.
▶ the fall into sin.
▶ redemption.
▶ re-creation.

The Reformed worldview recognizes a sovereign creating God who has made all things good, including people, who are are made in God's image. The fall into sin has corrupted and twisted all things in rebellion against God. God has come to redeem us in person in Jesus, who was completely God and completely man. Jesus paid the price for our sin on the cross and pours out his Holy Spirit on all who believe in him. The church is the body of Christ and is made up of those elected to carry out Christ's mission in the world until he comes again. This ministry of reconciliation looks forward to the re-creation when Jesus returns to make all things new, right every wrong, dry every tear, and heal every brokenness.

We live in the time between Christ's first coming and second coming—a time during which God is still personally active in our world. Jesus' words are still true: "My Father is always at his work to this very day, and I, too, am working" (John 5:17). Signs and wonders are one way that God is still working.

THE IMPACT OF OUR WORLDVIEW

ON OUR VIEW OF SIGNS AND WONDERS

Our view of signs and wonders is directly related to our understanding of who God is. In the Bible, we see a God who is infinite, almighty, able to do "immeasurably more than all we ask or imagine" (Eph. 3:20), completely wise and sovereign, and the overflowing fountain of all good. These beliefs draw a magnificent picture of God. We can go to this God with every need of our lives, recognizing that all good flows from him.

But our view of signs and wonders is also influenced by our understanding of the spiritual realm—of Satan, angels, demons, and evil spirits. Certainly the worldview of most of those living during the time of the Old and New Testament included the belief that other gods and spiritual beings existed. From the Garden of Eden in Genesis to the New City in Revelation, God's Word speaks of the reality of Satan and his attacks on God's people (Gen. 3; Job 1; John 8:44; 1 Peter 5:8; Rev. 12). Jesus' worldview recognized the direct involvement of Satan in people's lives. The exact relationship between these other "gods" and Satan is not clear, but they are all part of a spiritual realm that is in opposition to the true God. The Bible says that God sends angels as reinforcements in this spiritual realm. Throughout Scripture we see examples of angels

▶ serving God (Rev. 7:11-15).
▶ protecting God's people (Ex. 14:19; Ps. 91:11-12; Dan. 6:22; Acts 12:7).
▶ ministering to God's people (Gen. 16:7; 22:11; 1 Kings 19:5; Heb. 1:14).
▶ carrying out God's judgment (Gen. 19:1; Judg. 5:23; 2 Sam. 24:16; Acts 12:23; Rev. 15-16).
▶ fighting on God's behalf (Dan. 10:13).

Jesus himself is aware of the presence of angels, and he's ready for the regular attacks of Satan (Matt. 4; Mark 4:15; 8:33). His proclamation of the Word of God is accompanied by casting out demons as a demonstration of his victory over Satan (Matt. 8:16, 28). When it is time to send out his disciples, Jesus gives them authority to drive out evil spirits and to heal every disease and sickness (Matt. 10:1; Mark 16:15-18; Luke 10).

The apostle Paul also recognized a spiritual realm of beings that he calls "rulers . . . authorities . . . powers of this dark world . . . spiritual forces of evil in the heavenly realms" (Eph. 6:12) and "thrones or powers" (Col. 1:16). Paul also recognizes that Satan's servants "masquerade as servants of righteousness" (2 Cor. 11:15).

> We'll take a closer look at these powers in chapters 9-12.

ON MINISTRY AND MISSIONS

The worldview we adopt (consciously or unconsciously) has great implications for our missions and ministry.

Early on in my ministry in Paterson, New Jersey, a neighbor who was attending our church came to visit me. She wanted my help because she thought one of her husband's relatives had put a voodoo curse on her. I was totally unequipped to address the situation. Seminary didn't teach me how to deal with voodoo. I prayed with her, but did not begin to address the curse or a possible infestation of evil spirits. In fact, I wondered whether she needed a psychologist more than a preacher. My worldview and analytical theological training deterred me from ministering to her, and she suffered for years with severe physical, emotional, and psychological trauma that she attributed to the voodoo curse.

As a missionary to India, Paul Heibert found himself unable to deal with many of the ministry problems that arose because an awareness of the spirit realm was not part of his rationalistic worldview. In his classic article titled "The Flaw of the Excluded Middle" he writes:

> I had excluded the middle level of supernatural but this-worldly beings and forces from my own world view. . . . For me the middle zone did not really exist. Unlike Indian villagers, I had given little thought to spirits of this world, to local ancestors and ghosts or to the souls of animals.
> —*Missiology: An International Review,* Vol. X, No. 1, Jan., 1982, p. 43.

Hiebert identified in himself what he saw in Western Christianity—the denial of the existence of angels and demons and other supernatural forces active in the world today.

Building on Hiebert's insights, pastor and author Jeff Stam argues that a biblical worldview recognizes that there is constant interchanging and interaction between the realm of God, the realm of angels and demons, and the realm of people. Stam states:

> A biblical worldview can give us that critical balance between pure animism and a naturalistic Western worldview—not only because it offers a satisfactory compromise but because it offers truth in dealing with reality. We want to avoid a fatalistic animism that portrays all things spiritual as being impersonal, disallowing a personal creator God with whom we have a personal relationship. At the same time, we want to avoid a fatalistic naturalism that denies God or anything spiritual, leading us down a path that eventually proves to be meaningless and void of purpose.
> —*Straight Talk About Spiritual Warfare*, CRC Publications, 1999, p. 40.

Embracing the dimensions of the spiritual realm mentioned in the Bible paves the way for a powerful presentation and demonstration of the gospel. Bishop Lesslie Newbigin has stated that evangelical missionaries, unequipped to deal with the spiritual realm, have been one of the most secularizing forces in the world. Another missionary, Neuza Itioka, agrees with this accusation.

> The result of this inadequate view of spiritual reality is that missionaries implant a secularized kind of Christianity. We did away with what we called the superstitions of ignorant, uneducated people. As a result, many converts were forced back to their old ways of life because there was no place in their newly adopted Christian worldview for the supernatural power they saw at work on a daily basis. This is tragic because it is at this juncture that the Holy Spirit is supposed to be at work.
> —"Mission in the 1990s: Two Views." *International Bulletin of Missionary Research*, Vol. 14, No. 1, Jan., 1990, p. 9.

Richard De Ridder, one of my Calvin Seminary professors and a missionary for many years to Sri Lanka, spoke of how irrelevant traditional Reformed theology seemed in Sri Lanka. Questions about Satan, demons, angels, and charms were of prime importance to Christians there. De Ridder writes: "Among the greatest joys that we experienced was to proclaim to men the victory of Christ over the powers and see the shackles of slavery to elemental spirits broken by Christ" (*Discipling the Nations,* Baker Book House, 1975, p. 222).

ON REFORMED THEOLOGY

The theology of Reformed Christians has also been affected by the pervading worldview. Former missionary and mission executive Eugene Rubingh spoke about this at the 1998 conference on "Kingdom Power and Evangelism":

> Our world view persuades us to practically omit evidence of God's immediacy, of his power over the sick, the possessed, the destitute. Now we who brought the message of Jesus Christ to our fellows in the third world may learn from them the truth that the cosmic conflict takes place all around and in us and that the Lord will win.
> —"Kingdom and Power and Theology," Church Development Resources, Christian Reformed Home Missions, 1988, p. 11.

The roots of the rationalistic approach can be found in the reaction of the Reformation to some of the Roman Catholic "supernaturalism." Reformers did their best to eliminate exorcism, gifts of healing, and miracles. But by concentrating on God's majesty and holiness, Reformers somewhat lost sight of God's personal interest and touch.

The Calvinist emphasis on God's divine decrees can also make God seem unmovable and unresponsive to our prayers. But God is not a distant dictator uninvolved in daily affairs or an occasional visitor who only appears in spectacular ways. As John Calvin recognized, there is an intricate relationship between the sovereignty of God and the power of Satan and sin. Calvin encouraged believers in their struggle against Satan while recognizing that God is still in control.

As the Christian church carries out the great commission to bring the gospel to all nations, it is vital that we examine whether we are bringing the whole gospel or a culturally conditioned and limited gospel. Earlier missionary mistakes of American colonialism may be continuing if we teach an impotent American Christianity. As American worldviews about God and Satan change to embrace New Age and post-modern worldviews, we must ask if we are proclaiming the full gospel of Jesus Christ in all its power to address these new deceptions of Satan.

WHAT ABOUT *OUR* WORLDVIEW?

John Calvin spoke of the Scriptures as "spectacles" that clearly show us the true God (*Institutes of the Christian Religion,* The Westminster Press, 1960, p. 69). Because each person looks through the spectacles of his or her own cultural background, people may see very different things when they read the same Scriptures. If we are to exegete and read the Scriptures correctly, it is vital that we are aware of our own presuppositions and cultural "baggage." We need to discern and question accepted worldviews. At times, because of our lack of openness, we may miss seeing some of the work and blessings of God. God spoke to Isaiah saying: "As the heavens are higher than the earth, so are my ways higher than your ways, and my thoughts than your thoughts" (Isa. 55:9). We often want to completely understand God's way, but we must come to the point of accepting that God will do what he wills. God calls us to be obedient, and we must never let our own expectations put limits on God. As we let go of our presuppositions, we can begin anew to recognize and live in the power that Christ poured out through the Holy Spirit. We can practice that power in worship, evangelism, prayer, and the confrontation of evil at all levels. It's hard for most people to change their thinking, but doing so can affect the ways we worship, pray for people, confront evil and sin, confront evil spirits and demonic activity, evangelize unbelievers, and fellowship with fellow Christians.

John Wimber, one of the early leaders of the signs and wonders movement, insists that

> Western Christians must undergo a shift in perception to become involved in a signs and wonders ministry, a shift toward a worldview that makes room for God's miraculous intervention. It is not that we allow God's intervention; he does not need our permission. The shift is that we begin to see his miraculous works and allow them to affect our lives.

May we be able to join the Christians of the New Testament church with expectation, and perhaps some fear and trembling, in their prayer: "Now Lord, consider their threats and enable your servants to speak your work with great boldness. Stretch out your hand to heal and perform miraculous signs and wonders through the name of your holy servant Jesus" (Acts 4:29-30).

TESTIMONIES FROM . . .

PAUL LEWIS (1973)

His eyes were glassy, his clothes ragged, his hair matted, and he was desperate. "I'm going to kill this animal," he repeated three times. A demon in a man trapped in spiritism was challenging the crowd of people around him, including an evangelical missionary. I remembered the words of Jesus, "Behold, I give you power over all the power of the enemy, and nothing by any means shall hurt you." I felt I should rebuke the demon in the name of Jesus, but what if nothing happened? All the people gathered would ridicule me. I slipped behind another man and watched as the man finally got up and started down the street being held by two men. Abruptly he threw them off and started running. . . . There I was—a defeated missionary in the interior of Brazil, ready to pack up and go home. When face to face with the enemy, I was afraid. Who had told me how to deal with demons?

—*Attack from the Spirit World*, Tyndale Press, 1973, pp. 203-204.

JOHN G. PATON, AS TOLD BY BILLY GRAHAM (1975)

The Reverend John G. Paton, a missionary in the New Hebrides Islands, tells a thrilling story involving the protective care of angels. Hostile natives surrounded his mission headquarters one night, intent on burning the Patons out and killing them. John Paton and his wife prayed all during that terror-filled night that God would deliver them. When daylight came they were amazed to see the attackers unaccountably leave. They thanked God for delivering them. A year later, the chief of the tribe was converted to Jesus Christ, and Mr. Paton, remembering what had happened, asked the chief what had kept him and his men from burning down the house and killing them. The chief replied in surprise, "Who were all those men you had with you there?" The missionary answered, "There were no men there; just my wife and I." The chief argued that they had seen many men standing guard—hundreds of big men in shining garments with drawn swords in their hands. They seemed to circle the mission station so that the natives were afraid to attack. Only then did Mr. Paton realize that God had sent his angels to protect them. The chief agreed that there was no other explanation.

—*Angels, God's Secret Agents*, Doubleday, 1975, p. 3.

M. SCOTT PECK (1983)

Five years ago when I began work on this book I could no longer avoid the issue of the demonic. . . . Having come over the years to a belief in the reality of benign spirit, or God, and a belief in the reality of human evil, I was left facing an obvious intellectual question: Is there such a thing as evil spirit? Namely, the devil? I thought not. In common with 99 percent of psychiatrists and the majority of clergy, I did not think the devil existed. Still, priding myself on being an open-minded scientist, I felt I had to examine the evidence that might challenge my inclination in the matter. . . . So I decided to go out and look for a case. . . . The third case turned out to be the real thing. The vast majority of cases described in the literature are those of possession by minor demons. These two were highly unusual in that both were cases of Satanic possession. I now know Satan is real. I have met it. . . . There is no way I can translate my experience into your experience. It is my intent, however, that as a result of my experience, closed-minded readers will become more open-minded in relation to the reality of evil spirits.

—*People of the Lie*, Simon & Schuster, 1983, pp.183-184.

REFORMED REFLECTIONS

NICENE CREED
We believe in one God,
   the Father almighty,
   maker of heaven and earth,
   of all things visible and invisible.
And in one Lord Jesus Christ,
   the only Son of God,
   begotten from the Father before all ages,
     God from God,
     Light from light,
     true God from true God,
   begotten, not made;
   of the same essence as the Father.
   Through him all things were made. . . .
And we believe in the Holy Spirit,
   the Lord, the giver of life.
   He proceeds from the Father and the Son,
   and with the Father and the Son is worshiped and glorified.
   He spoke through the prophets. . . .

Reflect on how your view of the world affects what you believe.

THE HEIDELBERG CATECHISM, Q&A 34
  Q. Why do you call him "our Lord"?
  A. Because—
     not with gold or silver,
     but with his precious blood—
   he has set us free
     from sin and from the tyranny of the devil,
   and has bought us,
     body and soul,
   to be his very own.

> Reflect on how believing that Jesus is "our Lord"
> affects how we view the world.

QUESTIONS TO THINK ABOUT

▸ Explain in your own words how God is "three in one." Observe how your worldview affects your explanation.

▸ What does it mean to you to be "set free from sin and from the tyranny of the devil"?

▸ How do science and reason affect how you interpret the Bible?

▸ Reflect on the difficulty you may have had in understanding someone from another culture. How did your worldviews differ? How did it affect your relationship?

PRAYER AND PRACTICE

Praise God for his abundant goodness and sing of his righteousness on a regular basis this week.

Pray aloud David's psalm of praise:

I will exalt you, my God the King;
I will praise your name for ever and ever.
Every day I will praise you
and extol your name for ever and ever.
Great is the LORD and most worthy of praise;
his greatness no one can fathom.
One generation will commend your works to another;
they will tell of your mighty acts.
They will speak of the glorious splendor of your majesty,
and I will meditate on your wonderful works.
They will tell of the power of your awesome works,
and I will proclaim your great deeds.
They will celebrate your abundant goodness
and joyfully sing of your righteousness.

The LORD is gracious and compassionate,
slow to anger and rich in love.
The LORD is good to all;
he has compassion on all he has made.

All you have made will praise you, O LORD;
your saints will extol you.
They will tell of the glory of your kingdom
and speak of your might,
so that all men may know of your mighty acts
and the glorious splendor of your kingdom.
Your kingdom is an everlasting kingdom,
and your dominion endures through all generations.

—Psalm 145:1-13

ADDITIONAL RESOURCES

BOOKS

▶ Long, Zeb Bradford and Douglas McMurry. *The Collapse of the Brass Heaven.* Grand Rapids, Mich.: Chosen Books, 1994.

▶ Sire, James W. *The Universe Next Door.* Downers Grove, Ill.: InterVarsity Press, 1988.

▶ Grenz, Stanley J. *A Primer on Postmodernism.* Grand Rapids, Mich.: William B. Eerdmans, 1996.

CHAPTER THREE

PURPOSES AND RESULTS OF SIGNS AND WONDERS

YOUR HANDS, O LORD, IN DAYS OF OLD
WERE STRONG TO HEAL AND SAVE;
THEY TRIUMPHED OVER PAIN AND DEATH,
O'ER DARKNESS AND THE GRAVE.
TO YOU THEY WENT, THE BLIND, THE MUTE,
THE PALSIED AND THE LAME,
THE LEPER SET APART AND SHUNNED,
THE SICK AND THOSE IN SHAME.

AND THEN YOUR TOUCH BROUGHT LIFE AND HEALTH,
GAVE SPEECH AND STRENGTH AND SIGHT;
AND YOUTH RENEWED, WITH HEALTH RESTORED,
CLAIMED YOU, THE LORD OF LIGHT.
AND SO, O LORD, BE NEAR TO BLESS,
ALMIGHTY NOW AS THEN,
IN EVERY STREET, IN EVERY HOME,
IN EVERY TROUBLED FRIEND.

O BE OUR MIGHTY HEALER STILL,
O LORD OF LIFE AND DEATH;
RESTORE AND STRENGTHEN, SOOTHE AND BLESS
WITH YOUR ALMIGHTY BREATH.
ON HANDS THAT WORK AND EYES THAT SEE,
YOUR HEALING WISDOM POUR,
THAT WHOLE AND SICK AND WEAK AND STRONG
MAY PRAISE YOU EVERMORE.

—Edward H. Plumptre, 1866, alt.

I still remember listening to the personal testimony of John Wimber, founder of the Vineyard movement, who is now at home with the Lord. A former rock musician and drug addict, he was born again by the Spirit of God through reading about the life of Jesus. He began attending a local church and after a few weeks had this conversation with the pastor:

"When are you going to do it?"
"Do what?" asked the pastor.
"Do what Jesus did," said Wimber. "Heal the sick, raise the dead, cast out demons."
"Oh," said the pastor. "We don't do that any more."
"Don't do that any more?" responded a shocked Wimber. "What do you mean, 'you don't do that any more'?"

Wimber went on to be one of the leaders of what has become known as the "third wave of the Holy Spirit," with an emphasis on signs and wonders.

This chapter will give an overview of purposes for signs and wonders and the results of signs and wonders in the Bible. We'll note how signs and wonders

▸ proclaim the Word of God.
▸ demonstrate the presence of the kingdom of God.
▸ demonstrate the power of the Holy Spirit.
▸ testify to the power of prayer.
▸ give evidence of our faith in Jesus.
▸ defeat the devil.

In chapters 4-9 we will study each of these six purposes more closely and think about their significance for Christians today.

Purpose 1: Proclaiming the Word of God

Biblical preaching has always been one of the hallmarks of the Reformed faith. When I was ordained, I became known as a "minister of the Word." We believe true preaching from the Word of God is God still speaking today.

The biblical signs and wonders that we examined in chapter 1, along with other Old Testament and New Testament miracles, were often visible manifestations accompanying the written or spoken Word of God.

For example, when God told Moses to go speak to the Israelites, God gave Moses signs to accompany the message. Most of Jesus' miracles were done in the context of teaching and preaching (Luke 7:21-22). The seventy-two disciples were commissioned by Jesus to "heal the sick . . . and tell them, 'The kingdom of God is near you'" (Luke 10:9). Jesus himself referred to his miracles as confirmation of his relationship to the Father (John 10:38), and the disciples saw his miracles as proof that Jesus was the Son of God (Acts 2:22).

In the book of Acts, signs and wonders were closely related to the evangelistic growth of the church through the proclamation of the Word of God. Paul also considered signs, wonders, and miracles to be "the things that mark an apostle" (2 Cor. 12:12) and confirm the messenger of God. Signs and wonders proclaimed and demonstrated the Word of God.

Reformed folk have traditionally believed that such miracles were limited strictly to the apostolic age, as a way of spreading the gospel until the written Word of God was confirmed in the canon of Scripture. Signs and wonders encouraged faith, validated the spoken Word of God and the messengers of God, and proved Christ's divinity. John Calvin taught that these miraculous powers have ceased (*Institutes of the Christian Religion*, The Westminster Press, 1960). Calvin's conclusion may be more a theological deduction of his time in history than a correct biblical exegesis. (We will explore Calvin's position further in chapter 4.)

Although signs and wonders did serve to confirm the messenger and the Word of God, they were also a response to the Word of God. Moses was initially given signs to confirm his credibility to the Israelites and the Egyptians. The later plagues and the Exodus went far beyond confirmation of Moses to the demonstration of God's Word and power.

When Jesus is asked for a sign to prove who he is, he refuses because his miracles were not for confirmation purposes alone. The miracles, by Jesus' own testimony, demonstrate his relationship to the Father." Do not believe me unless I do what my Father does. But if I do it even though you do not believe me, believe the miracles, that you may learn and understand that the Father is in me, and I in the Father" (John 10:38).

> We'll take a more in-depth look at Purpose 1 in chapter 4.

PURPOSE 2: DEMONSTRATING THE PRESENCE OF THE KINGDOM

A second biblical purpose for miracles, signs, and wonders is to proclaim the presence of the kingdom of God. Jesus repeatedly proclaimed, "The kingdom of God is near" (Luke 10:11), and, "the kingdom of God has come to you" (Luke 11:20). Jesus also cast out demons as a sign of his and the Father's power and victory over Satan. When people accused Jesus of being demon-possessed himself, Jesus responded, "If I drive out demons by the Spirit of God, then the kingdom of God has come upon you" (Matt. 12:28).

Jesus' teaching on the kingdom of God emphasized that God's rule had begun. In response to his disciples' request to teach them how to pray, Jesus told them to pray "your kingdom come" (Matt. 6:10). Question and Answer 123 of The Heidelberg Catechism expounds on this theme:

Q. What does the second request [of the Lord's Prayer] mean?

A. *Your kingdom come* means,

Rule us by your Word and Spirit in such a way
    that more and more we submit to you.

Keep your church strong, and add to it.

Destroy the devil's work;
destroy every force which revolts against you
and every conspiracy against your Word.

Do this until your kingdom is so complete and perfect
that in it you are
all in all.

For centuries theologians have suggested that the kingdom of God is "already" present but "not yet" complete. The rule of Christ has started and will be completed at his second coming. This understanding of the present kingdom of Christ is a good basis for understanding the continued manifestation of signs and wonders. They are visible evidences of the kingdom of God that is already present—signposts of hope and symbols of the truth of the promises and providence of God.

Miracles are also visible demonstrations of God's sincere care and compassion for very real human needs. Jesus cared that people were hungry, crippled, deaf, blind, and dying. He cured them because of his compassion. When he heard two blind men shouting at him from the side of the road, "Jesus had compassion on them and touched their eyes. Immediately they received their sight and followed him" (Matt. 20:34). Jesus' miracles were also done so that those who were healed would experience the power of God in their lives. When questioned why a certain man had been born blind, Jesus responded, "This happened so that the work of God might be displayed in his life" (John 9:3).

We'll take a more in-depth look at Purpose 2 in chapter 5.

PURPOSE 3: SHOWING THE POWER OF THE HOLY SPIRIT

In twenty-seven years of ministry in the city of Paterson, I have learned much about the work and power of the Holy Spirit from the pastors who, with me, have participated in Paterson Pastor's Worship. We all recognize that we could never do ministry and would never survive in ministry in a city like Paterson without the power of the Holy Spirit.

The Pentecostal outpouring of the Holy Spirit is another foundation for the continuation of signs and wonders today. Signs and wonders following the outpouring of the Holy Spirit show the Spirit's power *(exousia)* that Jesus promised to all believers (Acts 1:8). Luke records these miraculous demonstrations of the Spirit's power:

▸ the wind, fire, and languages of Pentecost (Acts 2:1-12)
▸ the gift of tongues at the conversion of the first Gentiles (10:45-46)
▸ the Spirit's transport of Philip to a new mission field following the conversion of the Ethiopian (8:39).

Throughout the Old and New Testaments we see the Holy Spirit

▸ preparing people for special tasks that they would otherwise be unable to complete (Ex. 31:3; Isa. 61:1; Acts 4:9-16).
▸ being poured out on God's restored people (Joel 2:28-29).
▸ leading unbelievers to obedience and faith (1 John 3:21-24).

The power of the Spirit is also demonstrated in the gifts the Spirit gives to the body of believers. Some of these gifts manifested themselves as signs and wonders. The purpose of *sign* gifts (such as tongues, interpretation, prophecy, message of knowledge and wisdom, healing, miracles) was to confirm a person as an apostle or disciple, proclaim the presence of the kingdom of God, and help the church grow.

For example, Philip's word of knowledge and angelic guidance about the Ethiopian on the desert road south of Jerusalem led to the baptism of the man who then brought the gospel to Africa. Paul states, "I will not venture to speak of anything except what Christ has accomplished through me in leading the Gentiles to obey God by what I have said and done— by the power of signs and miracles, through the power of the Spirit" (Rom. 15:18).

God's people can rejoice in and use all the gifts the Spirit has given. These gifts

▸ contribute to the common good of the body of Christ (1 Cor. 12:7).
▸ "prepare God's people for works of service so that the body of Christ may be built up" (Eph. 4:12).

▶ enable God's people to demonstrate God's grace to others (1 Pet. 4:10).

The early church in Acts demonstrates that when the gifts of the Spirit are used, God's church grows

▶ in numbers (Acts 2:41; 5:14).
▶ among new people and nations (8:5-8; 15:12).
▶ in discipleship among Christians as they speak the word of God boldly (4:31), experience Christian joy (8:8), and endure opposition and persecution (6:8-15).

We'll take a more in-depth look at Purpose 3 in chapter 6.

PURPOSE 4: TESTIFYING TO THE POWER OF PRAYER

Every Easter Sunday we gather with about ten churches of many denominations on top of the mountain that overlooks our city. We watch the sun rise, sing "He Lives," preach the Word of God, and pray over our city. As we lift our hands and voices over this city of more than 160,000 residents, we pray for salvation, deliverance, healing, wholeness, family restoration, jobs, education, and so on. Although we rarely see instant change, we continue to pray and continue to see signs of the kingdom throughout the year. God responds to the prayers of his people.

The Old Testament provides numerous examples of God's answers to prayer, often in the form of signs and wonders. Recall these striking examples:

▶ To stop the plague of hail, Moses stretched out his hands in prayer to the Lord (Ex. 9:29).
▶ As long as Moses held up his hands, the Israelites were victorious against the Amalekites (Ex. 17:9-13).
▶ In the battle against the Amorites, Joshua prayed that the sun would stand still, and it did (Josh. 10).

▸ Daniel and his friends prayed that God would reveal the mystery of Nebuchadnezzar's dream to Daniel, and "the mystery was revealed to Daniel in a vision" (Dan. 2:17-19).

Jesus taught his disciples that they would receive whatever they asked for in his name (Matt. 18:19-20; John 16:23-26). Our prayers must be in accord with the will and the purpose of God. In the book of Acts, we read that God's purpose in answering prayers through signs and wonders is for the spread of the gospel and growth in Christian discipleship. In Acts 4:30 we hear believers pray, "Stretch out your hand to heal and perform miraculous signs and wonders through the name of your holy servant Jesus." The result of that prayer was that the believers spoke the Word of God with great boldness. Along with the signs and wonders that God gave in answer to that prayer, we see the continued growth of the church.

David Bryant, founder of the Concert of Prayer movement, documents the relationship between prayer and the growth of the church in these words:

> Throughout history, concerted prayer movements have provided launching pads for major advances of Christ's Kingdom. This was certainly true with four major religious awakenings in our nation in the past two centuries. As God's people kept praying, each awakening overflowed into revitalized churches and denominations, significant social reforms, widespread evangelistic in-gatherings, and the creation of scores of new mission sending societies.
> —*Christ Is All*, New Providence Publishers, 2004, p. 383.

We'll take a more in-depth look at Purpose 4 in chapter 7.

PURPOSE 5: GIVING EVIDENCE OF OUR FAITH

Miracles are not only to help *produce* faith but are also the *result* of faith. Signs and wonders encourage and build faith but also take place where faith is evident.

For example, Bartimaeus receives his sight as a result of his faith, evidenced by Jesus' words: "Go, your faith has healed you" (Mark 10:52). James, referring to the faith of the elders, teaches that "the prayer offered in faith will make the sick person well" (James 5:15).

Jesus continually called his disciples to greater faith and rebuked them for lack of faith. In one instance Jesus attributes his disciples' inability to cast out a demon to a lack of faith and says, "I tell you the truth, if you have faith as small as a mustard seed, you can say to this mountain, 'Move from here to there' and it will move. Nothing will be impossible for you" (Matt. 17:20-21).

Faith is a vital part of Christian discipleship. Lack of it can quench the work of the Holy Spirit and limit the work of God in one's life. Jesus wants our faith to increase.

We'll look more in depth at Purpose 5 in chapter 8.

PURPOSE 6: DEFEATING THE DEVIL

Another purpose and result of signs and wonders is to defeat the devil. One of our church's favorite choruses is "Victory Is Mine." It's a song of testimony to our victory in Christ over Satan and the powers of darkness. It goes like this:

> Victory is mine, victory is mine.
> Victory today is mine.
> I told Satan get thee behind.
> Victory today is mine.
> —Dorothy Norwood and Alvin Darling, © Malaco Music
> and Kosciusko Music. Used by permission.

In Christ, we live in the victory over all the power of the evil one. We have the same authority that Jesus had when he said to Peter, "Get behind me, Satan!" (Matt. 16:23).

The name *Satan* means "accuser" or "adversary" (see Zech. 3:1), and *devil* means "slanderer." In Scripture, the devil is also referred to as

▸ the tempter (Matt. 4:3).
▸ Beelzebub, the prince of demons (Matt. 12:24).

- the prince of this world (John 12:31).
- the ruler of the kingdom of the air (Eph. 2:2).
- dragon and serpent (Rev. 12:3, 9).

The Bible tells us of Satan's rebellion and fall (Rev. 12:7-9). We are warned that his hosts are very powerful (Eph. 6:12) and that Satan disguises himself as "an angel of light" (2 Cor. 11:14). Jesus, God's own Son, was tempted by Satan (Matt. 4:1-11).

Over and over, the Bible warns us to beware of the evil works of the devil. Satan is notorious for being

- a liar and murderer (John 8:44).
- a schemer (2 Cor. 2:11).
- a blinder of unbelievers (2 Cor. 4:4).
- a roaring lion looking for someone to devour (1 Pet. 5:8).
- a destroyer (Rev. 9:11).

In the New Testament, Jesus confronted and cast out demons and evil spirits (Matt. 8:28-34; Mark 1:21-27; Luke 9:37-43). Emphasizing the presence of the kingdom, Jesus said, "If I drive out demons by the Spirit of God, then the kingdom of God has come upon you" (Matt. 12:28).

Jesus also empowered his disciples and sent them out "to preach and to have authority to drive out demons" (Mark 3:14). This authority was first given to the twelve disciples and then to seventy-two others. When they "returned with joy and said, 'Lord, even the demons submit to us in your name,'" Jesus replied, "I saw Satan fall like lightning from heaven" (Luke 10:17-18).

Paul recognized the power of Satan in the lives of unbelievers who "followed the ways of this world and the ruler of the kingdom of the air, the spirit who is now at work in those who are disobedient" (Eph. 2:2).

The Reformed confessions recognize a personal devil, who, along with his hosts, promotes unbelief and ungodliness and attacks the church. But most American Christians no longer believe that Satan and his hosts are actual spiritual beings. This lack of belief in a real devil and in evil spirits leaves Christians unready to confront their enemy.

We'll take a more in-depth look at Purpose 6 in chapter 9.

THE RESULTS OF
SIGNS AND WONDERS

Throughout the New Testament, we see the results of signs and wonders parallel to their purposes as

- ▸ the Word of God goes forth.
- ▸ the kingdom of God is established.
- ▸ the power of the Holy Spirit is at work.
- ▸ the prayers of God's people are answered.
- ▸ the faith of God's people is strengthened.
- ▸ Satan is defeated.

The final result of any miracle helps us understand if it was from God. The book of Acts provides an interesting case study. Each time signs and wonders are mentioned, specific results are noted. Consider a few examples:

- ▸ "After [the believers] prayed, the place where they were meeting was shaken. And they were all filled with the Holy Spirit and spoke the word of God boldly" (Acts 4:31).
- ▸ "More and more men and women believed in the Lord and were added to their number. . . . Crowds gathered . . . bringing their sick and those tormented by evil spirits, and all of them were healed" (5:14, 16).
- ▸ "When the crowds heard Philip and saw the miraculous signs he did, they paid close attention. . . . evil spirits came out of many, and many paralytics and cripples were healed. So there was great joy in [Samaria]" (8:6-7).
- ▸ "At Iconium Paul and Barnabas . . . spoke so effectively that a great number of Jews and Gentiles believed. But the Jews who refused to believe stirred up the Gentiles. . . . There was a plot . . . to mistreat [Paul and Barnabas]" (14:1-2, 5).
- ▸ At Ephesus "God did extraordinary miracles through Paul, so that even handkerchiefs and aprons that had touched him were taken to the sick, and their illnesses were cured and the evil spirits left them. . . . Many of those who believed now came and openly confessed their evil deeds. A number who had practiced sorcery brought their scrolls together and burned them publicly. . . . In this way the word of the Lord spread widely and grew in power" (19:11-12, 18-20).

In the book of Acts we see that the results of signs and wonders include the numerical growth of the church through conversions and the growth of Christians in discipleship. People are healed of illness and relieved from suffering. Evil spirits and demons are cast out, and superstitious beliefs are exposed and defeated. Joy comes to entire cities as a result of miracles. At the same time, opposition arises, and opportunists spread false teaching.

From this study, it is also evident that the result of signs and wonders is not the end of all human suffering and injustice. Some problems and oppression are alleviated, but we look forward with hope to the return of Christ, when God "will wipe every tear. . . . There will be no more death or mourning or crying or pain, for the old order of things [will have] passed away." And yet already Christ is beginning to make "everything new!" (Rev. 21:4-5).

The results of God-given signs and wonders may include personal spiritual growth within believers as well as corporate involvement in seeking God's justice, righteousness, and will for all people. External growth of the church occurs when the gospel is taken to all nations and as the rule of Christ in the world is upheld by believers through their obedience. Signs and wonders are given by God to his people to bring about these kinds of results. So it is that we join the early disciples in faithful work, obedience, and joyful celebration of demonstrations of God's power.

TESTIMONIES FROM . . .

EUSEBIUS PAMPHILUS (BISHOP OF CAESAREA C. A.D. 263-339?)

These accounts are given by Irenaeus (A.D.140-203) in those five books of his. . . . In the second book of the same work, he also shows that even down to his times, instances of divine and miraculous power were remaining in some churches. . . . Wherefore, also, those that were truly his disciples, receiving grace from him, in his name performed these things for the benefit of other men, as every one received the free gift from him. Some, indeed, most certainly and truly cast out demons, so that frequently those persons themselves that were cleansed from wicked spirits believed and were received into the church. Others have the knowledge of things to come, as also visions and prophetic communications; others heal the sick by the imposition of hands, and restore them to health. And, moreover, as we have said above, even the dead have been raised and continued with us many years. And why should we say more? It is impossible to tell the number of the gifts which the church throughout the world received from God, and the deeds performed in the name of Jesus Christ, that was crucified under Pontius Pilate, and this too every day for the benefit of the heathen, without deceiving any, or exacting their money.

—*The Ecclesiastical History of Eusebius Pamphilus,* translated by Christian Frederick Cruse, Baker Book House, 1958, pp. 186-187.

HANK POTT (1987)

I had just finished speaking at a businessmen's luncheon about God and Satan and spiritual warfare. Slowly the cluster of men drifted away, but one remained. Obviously agitated, he told me he had been oppressed by evil spirits for some time, specifically the spirits of violence and of child sacrifice. I knew I could not or should not handle this one on my own. I found a friend in the lobby, and others also agreed to join us. We began to pray for deliverance in Jesus' name. As our friend's eyes bulged and he started foaming at the mouth, he began to scream and yell, and we told the spirits to be quiet. Twenty minutes or so later, he collapsed in his chair and only very slowly opened his eyes and said in a whisper, "Praise God! Jesus has set me free!" We counseled him for a bit on how he could stay free. Did this take place in Africa? No, in Tacoma, Washington, sometime in the spring of 1985.

—"Lessons from Africa Warfare," *The Banner,* June 8, 1987, p. 8.

RICHARD DE RIDDER

Among the Muslim villages of a certain West African country, the local madman periodically terrorized everyone. He attacked people walking along lonely paths, set fire to homes, and sometimes destroyed crops. In between times, the man behaved in relatively normal fashion. But when he went on a rampage, nobody could control him or calm him down. Local sorcerers had tried to rid him of evil spirits, but nothing helped. Finally, after a particularly destructive episode in which the man injured several villagers and did considerable damage, the people came to a Christian missionary and asked if he had power to free the madman of the evil forces which drove him. The missionary agreed on a time, and with everyone gathered in a circle, he conducted a prayer session, which ended with a call that God would free the man permanently of the evil spirit. God answered the prayer, and the man never went on a rampage again. From that time on, the missionary noted a remarkable openness to the gospel in the villages of that region.

—*Let the Whole World Know*, Baker Book House, 1988, p. 117.

REFORMED REFLECTIONS

THE BELGIC CONFESSION, ARTICLE 13

We believe that this good God,
    after he created all things,
did not abandon them to chance or fortune
but leads and governs them
    according to his holy will,
in such a way that nothing happens in this world
without his orderly arrangement.

Yet God is not the author of,
nor can he be charged with,
the sin that occurs.
For his power and goodness
are so great and incomprehensible
that he arranges and does his work very well and justly
even when the devils and wicked men act unjustly.

We do not wish to inquire
    with undue curiosity
into what he does that surpasses human understanding
    and is beyond our ability to comprehend.
But in all humility and reverence
we adore the just judgments of God,
which are hidden from us,
    being content to be Christ's disciples,
so as to learn only what he shows us in his Word,
    without going beyond those limits.

Reflect on how it is "beyond our ability to comprehend"
when God chooses to do or not to do a miracle.

QUESTIONS TO THINK ABOUT

- ▸ Can the purposes of signs and wonders as we've described them in this chapter be accomplished in the church today without the actual manifestation of signs and wonders themselves? Explain.
- ▸ What is the relationship between what we do (preach the word, demonstrate the presence of the kingdom, receive the Holy Spirit, pray, believe in Jesus, resist the devil) and the signs and wonders that God does?
- ▸ Do you see any of the results that happened in the early church happening in your local church today? In the church worldwide? Why or why not?

PRAYER AND PRACTICE

Pray aloud Paul's prayer for the believers at Ephesus:

> I keep asking that the God of our Lord Jesus Christ, the glorious Father, may give you the Spirit of wisdom and revelation, so that you may know him better. I pray also that the eyes of your heart may be enlightened in order that you may know the hope to which he has called you, the riches of his glorious inheritance in the saints, and his incomparably great power for us who believe.
>
> —Ephesians 1:17-19

Practice opening "the eyes of your heart" in silence before the Lord. Write your experiences down in a journal or share with someone what God is showing you.

ADDITIONAL RESOURCES

BOOKS

- ▸ Dawson, John. *Taking Our Cities for God.* Lake Mary, Fla: Creation House, 1989.
- ▸ White, Thomas B. *The Believer's Guide to Spiritual Warfare.* Ann Arbor, Mich.: Servant Publications, 1990.

CHAPTER FOUR

PROCLAIMING
THE WORD OF GOD

AND NOW, O LORD, THIS MAN OF GOD,
WHO BREAKS THE BREAD OF LIFE THIS MORNING—
SHADOW HIM IN THE HOLLOW OF THY HAND,
AND KEEP HIM OUT OF THE GUNSHOT OF THE DEVIL.
TAKE HIM, LORD—THIS MORNING—
WASH HIM WITH HYSSOP INSIDE AND OUT,
HANG HIM UP AND DRAIN HIM DRY OF SIN.
PIN HIS EAR TO THE WISDOM-POST,
AND MAKE HIS WORDS SLEDGE HAMMERS OF TRUTH—
BEATING ON THE IRON HEART OF SIN.
LORD GOD, THIS MORNING—
PUT HIS EYE TO THE TELESCOPE OF ETERNITY,
AND LET HIM LOOK UPON THE PAPER WALLS OF TIME.
LORD, TURPENTINE HIS IMAGINATION,
PUT PERPETUAL MOTION IN HIS ARMS,
FILL HIM FULL OF THE DYNAMITE OF THY POWER,
ANOINT HIM ALL OVER WITH THE OIL OF THY SALVATION,
AND SET HIS TONGUE ON FIRE.

—James Weldon Johnson, "Listen, Lord—A Prayer,"
God's Trombones, Penguin Books, 1927, p. 14.
© 1927, Viking Press, Inc.; renewed © 1955, Grace Nail Johnson.
Used by permission of Viking Penguin, a division of Penguin Group (USA), Inc.

ur church's gospel choir sings one of my favorite songs, an old one called "We Need to Hear from You." A prayer sung to the Lord, it goes like this.

We need to hear from you,
Lord, we need a word from you.
If we don't hear from you Lord,
what will we do?

—Sandra Crouch, © 1982, Bud John Songs, Inc./
Crouch Music. Used by permission.

The proclamation of the Word of God has held a prominent place in our Reformed tradition. This chapter will explore the first purpose of signs and wonders: to proclaim the Word of God. We will see how signs and wonders confirm the Word of God and result from the proclamation of the Word of God.

BIBLICAL MESSENGERS OF THE WORD OF GOD

PROPHETS

In the Old Testament, the Word of God was proclaimed by God to the prophets. Miracles and signs and wonders sometimes accompanied that proclamation. When God spoke to Moses on Mount Sinai, the mountain was covered with smoke and trembled violently (Ex. 19). When Elijah confronted the prophets of Baal, the Lord's fire consumed the water-drenched altar with fire—stones and all—and God sent rain to end the drought (1 Kings 18). When God's Word was absent due to the people's disobedience, miracles were also absent. "We are given no miraculous signs; no prophets are left, and none of us knows how long this will be" (Ps. 74:9).

In the New Testament book of Acts, we meet the prophet Agabus who "through the Spirit predicted that a severe famine would spread over the entire Roman world" (Acts 11:28) and that Paul would be captured when he went to Jerusalem (21:10). Paul himself prophesied before a ship-wreck that all would be saved if they stayed on board (27:31).

Prophets are also referred to in Ephesians 4:11 as an ongoing office of the church to

> prepare God's people for works of service, so that the body of Christ may be built up until we all reach unity in the faith and in the knowledge of the Son of God and become mature, attaining to the whole measure of the fullness of Christ.

APOSTLES

In the New Testament, miracles and signs often accompany the proclamation of the Word and sometimes confirm the messenger: "Jesus of Nazareth was a man accredited by God to you by miracles, wonders and signs . . ." (Acts 2:22). Before Jesus ascended, he commissioned his disciples to preach, heal, teach, and cast out demons (Mark 16:15-18). At Pentecost, the Holy Spirit appeared on the apostles in tongues of fire and enabled them to preach in many languages (Acts 2).

In Reformed circles it has traditionally been taught that only apostles had the authority to perform miracles and signs and wonders. The word *apostle* is from the Greek word *apostolos*. This word has a variety of uses and translations but carries the general meaning of "sent out." In the New Testament, it is used with this meaning to refer primarily to the twelve disciples who were designated "apostles" (Mark 3:14). It is to these twelve that Jesus gave authority to "drive out all demons and cure diseases" (Luke 9:1) and to preach (9:6).

In Acts we're told that some of the first signs and wonders are done by the apostles (2:43, 5:12). But as the early church grows, miracles also accompany the ministry of the deacon Stephen (6:8) and the evangelist Philip (8:4). In Acts 14:14, Paul and Barnabas are designated as apostles. Paul implies that although his apostleship is not recognized by all, it is confirmed because he saw Jesus (1 Cor. 15:8-9) and because he did "the things that mark an apostle—signs, wonders and miracles" (2 Cor. 12:12).

PREACHERS

The apostolic calling of being a messenger is also captured in the Greek word *kerux*. A *kerux* is a herald, one who makes public proclamations on behalf of and under the authority of another. The verbal form conveys the meaning of announcing, proclaiming, making known. What is preached is the *euangelion* or "good news." The relationship between the preacher and the good news is illustrated in these words:

> How beautiful on the mountains are the feet of those who bring good news, who proclaim peace, who bring good tidings, who proclaim salvation, who say to Zion, "Your God reigns!"
> —Isaiah 52:7

In the New Testament, preaching is the primary means by which the good news is announced. Biblical preaching was at the forefront of the mission of the church in synagogues, on street corners, and in jails, fishing boats, bedrooms, living rooms, restaurants, bars, and hospitals. Preaching makes known

- "the good news" (Mark 16:15).
- "the good news of the kingdom of God" (Luke 8:1).
- "repentance and forgiveness of sins" (Luke 24:47).
- "the word of faith" (Rom. 10:8).
- Jesus' resurrection (1 Cor. 15:12).
- "Jesus Christ as Lord" (2 Cor. 4:5).

Jesus' preaching as well as the preaching of the disciples is often accompanied by signs and wonders.

EVANGELISTS

Our English word *evangelism* comes from the Greek word *euangelion* which, again, means "good news." Whereas churches today often separate preaching from evangelism, in the New Testament there was a close relationship between the two. As the gospel was preached in word and deed by God's people, the body of Christ grew. The gospel was to include both proclamation and demonstration, as Jesus revealed in his "inaugural address":

> The Spirit of the Lord is on me, because he has anointed me to preach good news to the poor. He has sent me to proclaim freedom for the prisoners, and recovery of sight for the blind, to release the oppressed, to proclaim the year of the Lord's favor.
> —Luke 4:18-19

This text clearly demonstrates the connection between the proclamation of the life-changing gospel and the miracles and signs and wonders that accompany it. When Jesus sent out his first class of evangelists-in-training, he said, "Heal the sick who are there and tell them, 'The kingdom of God is near you'" (Luke 10:9).

Biblical preaching of the gospel includes proclamation and demonstration. That demonstration can be in the form of miracles and signs and wonders as well as in acts of mercy, love, and service. Signs and wonders of one kind or another will accompany the true proclamation of God's Word.

THE AUTHORITY OF SCRIPTURE

One of the hallmarks of Reformed Christianity is its emphasis on the authority of Scripture. Article 5 of the Belgic Confession summarizes this Reformed position on the authority and sufficiency of Scripture (see also Article 7 at the end of this chapter):

> We receive all these books
> and these only
> as holy and canonical,
> for the regulating, founding and establishing
> of our faith.
>
> And we believe
> without a doubt
> all things contained in them—
> not so much because the church
> receives and approves them as such
> but above all because the Holy Spirit
> testifies in our hearts
> that they are from God,
> and also because they
> prove themselves
> to be from God.

In a classic report "The Nature and Extent of Biblical Authority," Synod 1972 of the Christian Reformed Church gave practical clarification of this doctrine. Related to the interpretation and application of Scripture, the report states:

> The divine authority of the Word of God is actually recognized only when one has submitted himself to the One of whom the Scripture speaks. Any understanding of the Word of God which does not use this center as the key for understanding its various parts, is erroneous, no matter how vigorously it affirms the inspiration and divine authority of the Scriptures.
>
> —*Acts of Synod 1972,* Christian Reformed Church
> in North America, 1972, p. 509.

The emphasis of this report is that Scripture must be understood from the perspective of a relationship with Jesus Christ, the Word made flesh. Knowledge of the Bible, teaching, and even preaching apart from this will be vain exercises. The Bible is God's special revelation to be applied daily. Written words become "good news" through their proclamation and demonstration by the Holy Spirit. In Reformed theology, this preaching is identified as one of the keys of the kingdom and is carried out by preachers. (See also Heidelberg Catechism Q&A 84 in "Reformed Reflections" at the end of this chapter.)

SPECIAL REVELATION AND THE APOSTOLIC AGE

Reformed theologians from John Calvin to B.B. Warfield taught that signs and wonders were the result of apostolic authority and therefore ended with the age of the apostles. Calvin taught that the purpose of miracles and healings was to get the gospel off the ground. Once we had the written Scriptures, Calvin believed, signs and wonders were no longer necessary. This *cessationist* view is what I was taught as a child without knowing it, and it is held by many in the Reformed community today.

A detailed study of the contrasting biblical arguments in this area can be found in the book *Are Miraculous Gifts for Today?* (Zondervan, 1996). Edited by Stanley N. Gundry, it explores the cessationist view, the "open but cautious" view, the third wave, and the Pentecostal/charismatic views.

It is my position that signs and wonders were not limited to the apostolic age since they were not even limited to the apostles alone. In Luke 10:1 we are told that seventy-two disciples were commissioned to proclaim the gospel in word and deed. Mark's version of the Great Commission in chapter 16 is addressed to more than just the traditional few apostles. Peter recognized that at Pentecost the Holy Spirit was poured out on all believers, fulfilling the prophecy of Joel: "In the last days, God says, I will pour out my spirit on all people. . . . I will show wonders in the heaven above and signs on the earth below..." (Acts 2:17,19).

I do not believe there is sufficient biblical evidence to suggest that the apostle Paul had any intention that the offices of apostle and prophet (Eph. 3:5) would end or that any of the gifts of miraculous powers and healing (1 Cor. 12:9-11) would cease. Rather, Paul clearly teaches that these were for the common good. The use of miracles, signs, and wonders to confirm the Word of God and the messenger of God still continues today.

Even Reformed theologian G.C. Berkouwer challenges the traditional Reformed cessationist view. He says,

> It is clear to us now, of course, that the special signs and miracles were not limited to the time of Christ's walk on earth. . . . But it is everywhere evident that these miracles do not occur to provide the Church with a supernatural means of self-protection. They are aimed at the establishment and extension of the kingdom in the world . . . we find nothing in the Scriptures to indicate a line that we can draw through a definite period to mark off a boundary between the time of miracles and the time of the absence of miracles.
> —*The Providence of God,* W. B. Eerdmans Publishing Co., 1952. p. 224.

THE HOLY SPIRIT AND SCRIPTURE

We also see that God still speaks his Word to us today through certain gifts of the Spirit. These gifts, often called *sign* gifts, are among the gifts that some believe have ended. The official position of my own denomination, the Christian Reformed Church, is that these gifts continue—a view arising out of an extensive synodical study report on Neo-Pentecostalism presented in 1973. These Word gifts include prophecy, word of knowledge, word of wisdom, tongues, and interpretation of tongues. It is important to recognize that when these Word gifts are used, God is not giving us a new revelation in addition to Scripture but is speaking in specific situations.

The apostle Paul speaks of these gifts in 1 Corinthians 12 and more extensively on prophecy in 1 Corinthians 13 and in Romans 12. Pastor and author Alvin J. Vander Griend defines these gifts as follows:

▸ Prophecy: The special Spirit-given ability to receive and communicate a message from God so that believers may be edified and encouraged and so that unbelievers may be convinced.
▸ Tongues: The special Spirit-given ability to speak in sounds and utterances previously unknown to the speaker.
▸ Interpretation of Tongues: The special Spirit-given ability to interpret into known language a message spoken in tongues.
▸ Knowledge: The special Spirit-given ability to receive from God knowledge that is crucial to ministry and that could not have been obtained in other ways.
▸ Wisdom: The special Spirit-given ability to see situations and issues from God's perspective and to apply God-given insights to specific areas of need.

—Discover Your Gifts and Learn How to Use Them, Student Manual, Faith Alive Christian Resources, 1996, pp. 125, 133, 109,141.

The question that often arises about these gifts is this: how does the revelation they bring compare to Scripture? Although we boldly confess the sufficiency of Scripture (see Belgic Confession, Art. 7), we also recognize the ongoing power and work of the Holy Spirit. As we have seen, we can only understand Scripture through the illumination of the Holy Spirit. The revelation character of these spiritual gifts is not equal to Scripture or in conflict with Scripture. They are given by the Holy Spirit for specific times and situations, and their revelation must be in accord with Scripture.

Some theologians and pastors have made a theological distinction between two Greek terms for *word*: *logos* and *rhema*. They understand *logos* to refer to the written Word of God or the Bible, which is the foundation of how we know God. *Rhema* is the current word that God continues to speak to people through spiritual gifts, angels, visions, dreams, and the promptings of the Holy Spirit.

David Yonggi Cho, pastor of the largest church in the world in Seoul, Korea, describes this as the "Word of God which God uses to impart faith about specific circumstances into a man's heart" (*The Fourth Dimension, Vol. I,* Bridge-Logos, p. 72). In distinction from the written Scriptures that give us the complete knowledge and understanding of God, the *rhema* word gives specific words of direction from God. Cho says, "Faith comes by hearing and hearing by *rhema.*" Cho argues that Peter would have never walked on water on his own, but because he received a *rhema* word from Jesus to walk on the water, he did so.

One of my greatest joys is to see the power of the Word of God changing people. I have witnessed this happening following a sermon as someone comes forward to receive Jesus as Lord and Savior. I have seen it happen as people are freed from the power of drug and alcohol addictions that have bound them. I have seen words of knowledge identify hurts that needed healing and sins that needed confessing.

Signs and wonders continue to accompany the proclamation and demonstration of the Word of God. In the same way, the Holy Spirit illumines the Scriptures to our hearts and minds and gives gifts that enable the church to continue to hear God speak. These gifts must always be tested against the Scriptures, but it is by the Scriptures that we know they are given. These gifts are in and of themselves "signs and wonders" of God at work.

So what do we do to receive these manifestations? We

- preach and teach the Word of God.
- eagerly desire spiritual gifts, including the gifts of prophecy, tongues, interpretation of tongues, knowledge, and wisdom.
- listen and respond to the voice of God.
- welcome the signs and wonders that God will do.

Testimonies from . . .

GEORGE WHITEFIELD (1740)

Preached at Nottingham [Pennsylvania] both morning and evening, with such demonstration of the Spirit and such a wonderful movement amongst the hearers as few ever saw before. I was invited thither, by some of the inhabitants, who had a good work begun amongst them, some time ago, by the ministry of Mr. Blair, the Messrs. Tennents and Mr. Cross, the last of which had been denied the use of the pulpit by one of his own brethren and was obliged to preach in the woods, where the Lord manifested forth His glory and caused many to cry out, "What shall we do to be saved?" It surprised me to see such a multitude gathered together, at so short a warning and in such a desert place. I believe there were near twelve thousand. I had not spoke long before I perceived numbers melting. As I proceeded, the influence increased, till, at last, (both in the morning and the afternoon), thousands cried out, so that they almost drowned my voice. Never did I see a more glorious sight. Oh what tears were shed and poured forth after the Lord Jesus. Some fainted; and when they had got a little strength, they would hear and faint again. Others cried out in a manner as if they were in the sharpest agonies of death. Oh what thoughts and words did God put into my heart! After I had finished my last discourse, I was so pierced, as it were, and overpowered with a sense of God's love, that some thought, I believe, I was about to give up the ghost. How sweetly did I lie at the feet of Jesus.

—George Whitefields's Journals, *The Banner of Truth Trust*, 1960, pp. 424-425.

TOM SKINNER (1959)

I motioned for silence and began to speak. I told of the broadcast—how the speaker had given me insight to truth I'd never heard before. I told them that I was convinced Jesus Christ had died for all the sins I'd ever committed and had given me everlasting life. "Last night, I asked him to come inside me and live in me. And he answered me." I said, ". . . I don't understand everything involved, but I know that Christ has taken up residence in my life. And based on that commitment, I can no longer responsibly lead the gang."

You could have heard a pin drop. No one spoke. No one even moved. I walked down the aisle and out into the night air, half expecting a knife to come tearing into my back or a bullet to dig into my flesh. But nothing. I walked out without one person raising a hand against me. I nearly shouted my thankfulness to God.

Two nights later I saw "The Mop" (number two man in the gang) on the street. He motioned to me and said, "Tom, I wanna talk to you. . . . You know the other night when you got up and walked out of that meeting, I was gonna really cut you up. I was all set to put my knife right in your back." "And why didn't you?" "I couldn't move," he said, his eyes growing wider. "It was like somebody was holding me back—like I was glued to my seat!" He licked his lips and continued, "And I talked to some of the other guys too. I wasn't the only one. They said the same thing—that something, or somebody, actually held them back in their seats. . . . What d'ya make of it, Tom?" he asked.

"I know that the Christ I've committed myself to isn't just some fictitious character who lived two thousand years ago . . . some nebulous spirit floating around in the air somewhere. I know now that Jesus Christ is alive! He's real!" . . . Standing on 153rd St. and McCombs Place [in New York City] . . . an ex-gang leader, a Christian less than 48 hours, led another gang member to Christ.

—*Black and Free*, Zondervan Publishing House, 1968, pp. 66-67.

GRESFORD CHITEMO (1973)

One day in 1973 I heard of Edmund John, a man of God who was the brother of Johnson Sepeku, then the archbishop of Tanzania [East Africa]. This man was being used by God to preach the gospel, and many were convicted and repented of their sins. He was also praying for those who had diseases, and they were being healed. . . . After three days of fasting and three nights of prayer came the time of preaching. As we came out of the church, we heard people crying and saw them shaking with evil powers, and we could barely quiet them. We all preached in turns. Edmund John preached a very simple, straightforward sermon on salvation. He told people that God offered the gift of healing as bait. People came to be healed of physical illness, but God wanted to save. The response to this sermon was good. . . . Edmund prayed in the name of Jesus, the King of Kings, the most powerful name, and all were freed. . . . Because the gospel preaching is accompanied by the work of the Holy Spirit and there are signs and wonders, the power in the name of the Lord is apparent. People come to be healed of diseases or freed of demons. After they are prayed for and healed, they are instructed and prepared for baptism. This gospel with its signs and miracles has caused many—Muslims, traditional people, and nominal Christians—to believe in the saving power of our Lord. As my experience has shown, the work of the Holy Spirit is truly marvelous.

—David F. Wells, *God the Evangelist*, William B. Eerdmans Publishing Co., 1987, pp. 115-116.

THE BELGIC CONFESSION, ARTICLE 7

We believe
that this Holy Scripture contains
the will of God completely
and that everything one must believe
to be saved
is sufficiently taught in it.
For since the entire manner of service
which God requires of us
is described in it at great length,
no one—

even an apostle
or an angel from heaven, as Paul says—
ought to teach other than
what the Holy Scriptures have
already taught us.
For since it is forbidden
to add to or subtract from the Word of God,
this plainly demonstrates
that the teaching is perfect
and complete in all respects.

Reflect on how you have tested with Scripture what you have heard
from the voice of God when making decisions in your life.

THE HEIDELBERG CATECHISM, Q&A 84

**Q. How does preaching the gospel
open and close the kingdom of heaven?**

A. According to the command of Christ:

The kingdom of heaven is opened
by proclaiming and publicly declaring
to all believers, each and every one, that,
as often as they accept the gospel promise in true faith,
God, because of what Christ has done,
truly forgives all their sins.

The kingdom of heaven is closed, however,
by proclaiming and publicly declaring
to unbelievers and hypocrites that,
as long as they do not repent,
the anger of God and eternal condemnation
rest on them.

God's judgment, both in this life and in the life to come,
is based on this gospel testimony.

> Reflect on how the Word of God can
> bring about the miracle of conversion.

QUESTIONS TO THINK ABOUT
▸ Is the miracle of conversion one of the signs and wonders? Why or why not?
▸ Read Acts 8:4-8. What happened when the Word was preached?
▸ How would your church respond if this happened on a Sunday morning?
▸ What do you expect the preaching of the Word to do?
▸ How are you listening to the voice of God?

PRAYER AND PRACTICE
Pray aloud these words of Paul to the "holy and faithful brothers in Christ at Colosse":

> For this reason, since the day we heard about you, we have not stopped praying for you and asking God to fill you with the knowledge of his will through all spiritual wisdom and understanding. And we pray this in order that you may live a life worthy of the Lord and may please him in every way: bearing fruit in every good work, growing in the knowledge of God, being strengthened with all power according to his glorious might so that you may have great endurance and patience, and joyfully giving thanks to the Father, who has qualified you to share in the inheritance of the saints in the kingdom of light. For he has rescued us from the dominion of darkness and brought us into the kingdom of the Son he loves, in whom we have redemption, the forgiveness of sins.
>
> —Colossians 1:9-13

Look for an opportunity to share God's Word with someone this week. Pray that the Lord will help you recognize the opportunity when it comes.

ADDITIONAL RESOURCES

BOOKS

▸ Johnson, Ben Campbell. *The God Who Speaks*. Grand Rapids, Mich.:
William B. Eerdmans Publishing Co., 2004.
▸ Willard, Dallas. *Hearing God*. Downers Grove, Ill.: InterVarsity Press,
1999.

CHAPTER FIVE

DEMONSTRATING THE PRESENCE OF THE KINGDOM OF GOD

GOD'S GOT A KINGDOM.
GOD'S GOT A KINGDOM.
GOD'S GOT A KINGDOM,
BUT THE DEVIL'S GOT A KINGDOM TOO.
I'M GONNA PRAY-SING-PLANT-STUDY-BUY-VOTE
THAT DEVIL'S KINGDOM DOWN.
I'M GONNA PRAY-SING-REAP-STUDY-SELL-VOTE
THAT DEVIL'S KINGDOM DOWN
'CAUSE I HEARD THE VOICE OF JESUS SAY,
"SATAN, YOUR KINGDOM MUST COME DOWN.
SATAN, YOUR KINGDOM MUST COME DOWN."
ARE YOU LIVING IN THE KINGDOM?
ARE YOU LIVING IN THE KINGDOM?
ARE YOU LIVING IN THE KINGDOM?
THEN YOU KNOW YOU GOT A JOB TO DO.
YOU GOTTA PRAY-SING-VOTE-PLANT-BUY-STUDY
THAT DEVIL'S KINGDOM DOWN
'CAUSE YOU HEARD THE VOICE OF JESUS SAY,
"SATAN, YOUR KINGDOM MUST COME DOWN.
SATAN, YOUR KINGDOM MUST COME DOWN."

—Bill Evenhouse, *God's Got a Kingdom*,
Music Ministries of Nigeria, 1990. Permission sought.

My favorite part of the Lord's Prayer is the second petition: "your kingdom come" (Matt. 6:10). As I pray this, I pause and think about what it would look like in my Paterson neighborhood. What I see becomes my prayer: no injustice, no racism, no unemployment, no slum housing, no crime, no drive-by shootings, no AIDS, no drug dealers on the corners. I see children succeeding in school, strong marriages, whole families, meaningful work, decent homes, people in love with God and caring for each other. It sounds optimistic, but this is what Jesus tells us to pray for now "on earth as it is in heaven."

A few years ago, Stafford Miller, my prayer partner and pastor of St. Philips United Methodist Church, had a "biblical awakening" to the presence of the kingdom of God here and now. He immediately went out and had large banners made that now drape down his church building. The banners say, "We declare—the kingdom of God is here." This is a powerful proclamation in one of the poorest and toughest neighborhoods of our city. His ministry has changed as a result of this "biblical Reformed" discovery.

The biblical teaching on the kingdom of God is an important foundation for understanding the continued place and purpose of signs and wonders in the life of the Christian church and world today. In this chapter we will explore the second purpose of signs and wonders: to demonstrate the presence of the kingdom of God. We will

▸ formulate a biblical definition of the kingdom of God.
▸ examine what it means that the kingdom of God is present now on earth.
▸ see how the presence of the kingdom affects our lives, especially as it relates to signs and wonders.

KINGDOM—A BIBLICAL DEFINITION

The kingdom of God is a primary theme throughout the Old and New Testaments. It also holds a unique emphasis in Reformed theology. Let's explore this theme and work toward a definition.

KINGDOM IN THE OLD TESTAMENT
Although the phrase *kingdom of God* does not occur in the Old Testament, the idea of God's rule and reign is found throughout. Many passages refer to God's present rule over Israel (Isa. 43:15) and the

whole earth (Ps. 99:1-4; 103:19). Other passages refer to the future when God will be King (Isa. 24:23; Isa. 60; Zech.14). The prophecies of the Messiah (Isa. 40; 60) are closely related to the kingdom, since the Messiah would usher it in.

Old Testament scholar John Bright sums up the Old Testament teaching about the kingdom like this:

> We have seen . . . the concomitant hope of the consummation of God's purpose and the establishment of his Kingdom. Although this hope took many and various forms, it was always one hope. And although it was many times cruelly frustrated, it was never given up. . . . As long as Israel retained any sense of calling as the people of God, or any faith in the integrity and power of that God who is Lord of history, so long would there live the lively expectation of his coming Kingdom.
> —*The Kingdom of God*, Abingdon Press, 1953, p. 187.

KINGDOM IN THE NEW TESTAMENT

The word for *kingdom* in the New Testament is the Greek word *basileia*. This word means "rule," "reign," "royalty," or simply "kingdom." Although we usually think of a kingdom as a geographic place, the emphasis here is on the royal rule and royal power of the king. The phrase *kingdom of God* or *kingdom of heaven* is first used by John the Baptist as he announces that "the kingdom of heaven is near" (Matt. 3:2). Jesus' first words recorded in the gospel of Mark are about the kingdom: "The time has come. . . . The kingdom of God is near. Repent and believe the good news!" (Mark 1:15).

Throughout the four gospels we see that the kingdom is not only taught but also brought by Jesus. Jesus ushers in the kingdom (Matt. 4:17, 23; Luke 4:18-21). In Matthew 13, Jesus teaches what the kingdom of heaven is like in the parables of the sower, the mustard seed, the yeast, the hidden treasure, and the net. In response to John the Baptist's question if he was the Messiah, Jesus responded,

> "Go back and report to John what you have seen and heard: The blind receive sight, the lame walk, those who have leprosy are cured, the deaf hear, the dead are raised and the good news is preached to the poor."
> —Luke 7:22

KINGDOM—HERE AND NOW

KINGDOM COME

Some time ago I joined the youth of our church on a mission service trip to Whitesburg, Kentucky. In the heart of the Appalachian Mountains, this place so astounded the first settlers with its beauty that they named the valley "Kingdom Come."

Although Christians have repeatedly tried to identify the kingdom of God with a place, biblically it is defined as God's rule over all places. Jesus repeatedly proclaimed, "The kingdom of God is near you" (Luke 10:9) and "has come upon [or to] you" (Matt. 12:28; Luke 11:20). Jesus taught that the kingdom of God—God's rule—is now.

George Eldon Ladd explains this well:

> The most distinctive fact in Jesus' proclamation of the kingdom was its presence in breaking into history in his own person and mission. We should not be surprised to find *basileia tou theou* used of a new realm of redemptive blessing into which men enter by receiving Jesus' message about the kingdom of God.
> —*A Theology of the New Testament,* William B. Eerdmans Publishing Co., 1974, p. 70.

The kingdom was often misunderstood by the Jewish people of the Old Testament, by the zealots, and even by Jesus' own disciples. The zealots saw the kingdom as a place—Zion—and sought to usher it in through political and military means, with the Messiah leading this revolution. Jesus' disciples were also looking for a geographical and political kingdom. After spending three years with Jesus and witnessing his resurrection, they still did not understand what Jesus meant by the kingdom of God. This is evident in their question to Jesus just prior to his ascension: "Lord, are you at this time going to restore the kingdom to Israel?" (Acts 1:6). They were unable to recognize that Jesus was not restoring the kingdom to Israel but that he had ushered in a new kingdom—the kingdom of God.

The ascension of Jesus and the outpouring of the Holy Spirit firmly established God's kingdom on earth as in heaven. It also marked the condemnation of Satan (John 16:11). The disciples preached the present reality of the kingdom (Rom. 14:17; 2 Pet. 1:11) and also the future inheritance of the kingdom (2 Tim. 4:18). Jesus spoke of this future completion of the kingdom as the final culmination of all things at his return (Luke 13:29; Matt. 25).

KINGDOM CONFLICTS

Throughout church history, Christians have struggled to understand and apply the meaning of the kingdom of God to their lives. Constantine sought to establish the kingdom of God by demanding that all citizens of the Holy Roman Empire become Christians. The Crusades sought to establish the kingdom through the annihilation of Muslims and the recapturing of Jerusalem. John Calvin sought to make Geneva a model of the kingdom of God in all its religious, political, social, and economic structures. Later, the Puritans modeled this Reformed emphasis by trying to establish the kingdom of God in New England.

Each of these attempts to establish the kingdom of God met with varying degrees of success. Most failed to recognize that the kingdom of God is not bound to geographic territory but that it is present when the rule and reign of God are established.

The Heidelberg Catechism's answer to the meaning of the second request of the Lord's Prayer (see "Reformed Reflections" at the end of this chapter) stresses this Reformed understanding of the kingdom. The kingdom of God is the rule of God that is established by Christ's church.

Although the reality of Christ's kingdom may be recognized, its opposition to Satan's kingdom is often overlooked. In the classic work *Christ and Time* (Westminster John Knox, 1964), Oscar Cullman illustrates this with the example of D-Day and V-Day. In World War II, the Allies' victory on D-Day decided the outcome of the war, but the skirmishes continued and the enemy fought even harder until V-Day. We live in the time between when Christ won the decisive battle on the cross (D-Day) and when the victory will be finally complete (V-Day).

David F. W. Wells puts it another way:

> It is as if two people were playing chess. At a certain point, one of the players rises from the table, leaving his opponent to ponder his next move. The opponent struggles with all the possibilities because he is determined to win. What he has not realized is that there are only a limited number of moves that he can make, and not one of them can change the outcome of the game. No matter what he does, he will lose. Just so at the Cross, the outcome of the chess game between God and Satan

was decided. God will certainly win. Satan, however is presently playing out every conceivable option, imagining that somehow his rebellion will triumph. It will not.

—*God the Evangelist,* William B. Eerdmans
Publishing Co., 1987, p. 67.

Jesus proclaimed and demonstrated the presence of his kingdom by defeating Satan and invading his territory when he healed the sick, raised the dead, and cast out demons.

Herman Ridderbos, in his classic work *The Coming of the Kingdom* (The Presbyterian and Reformed Publishing Co., 1975, p. 67) concludes that Jesus proved "that Satan's power has been broken and that the kingdom has come." It was while reading this book that my prayer partner Stafford Miller, whom I mentioned earlier in this chapter, was awakened to the presence of the kingdom that has transformed his ministry. In one of the worst neighborhoods of Paterson, his ministry is a proclamation and demonstration of the presence of the kingdom of God through several holistic ministries that pray for healing for physical illness and institutional injustice, cast demons out of individuals and possessed structures, pray drug dealers off corners and into worship, and lead the homeless from the church's soup kitchen to wholeness in their "House of Promise."

KINGDOM—IN OUR LIVES

CHRISTIANS IN THE KINGDOM

Jesus still works on the stage of earthly history through his body, the church. Satan continues to attack God's rule through demons, sickness, death, and sin in all its forms. As Jesus defeated Satan and restored God's rule in these areas through exorcism, healing, raising the dead and conversions, so he will continue to bring restoration through his body, the church. Embracing Christ's authority in the present victory of his kingdom equips Christians for battle in the world.

Because God's kingdom is not yet complete, our authority is limited. That's why those living the new life in Christ still struggle with sin. These limitations should not deter us from obeying Jesus' command. The church still continues to do evangelism even though not everyone we reach out to comes to Christ. Though not everyone we pray for is healed, we continue to pray for healing.

The establishment of the kingdom includes the redemption of sin-sick souls as well as the restoration of sick and demon-possessed bodies. The signs and wonders of conversion, healing, and exorcism performed by Jesus and the apostles are dynamic incursions of the rule of God into the territory of Satan. They are not evidence of some charismatic talent, but demonstrations of the breaking in of the kingdom of God into time.

ALREADY—NOT YET

The future fulfillment of the kingdom breaks into the present. The future hope of Revelation 21 reaches into the present realities of our lives as the kingdom of God is established. The presence of God is manifest; death, sickness, suffering and pain are gone. G. E. Ladd explains this as the church living "between the times." The kingdom is already present but not yet complete. This biblical truth has tremendous implications for how we do ministry on personal and corporate levels.

Sometimes signs and wonders of the kingdom are demonstrated in personal ways. But it is important to realize that they are also demonstrated in corporate ways that relate to issues of injustice, racism, oppression, poverty, war, and economic exploitation. Signs and wonders of the present kingdom of God include more than the lengthening of someone's leg or the healing of someone's cancer. They must also be sought in the social, political, and economic power structures that affect the lives of millions.

Signs and wonders that declare the presence of the kingdom of God include

- healing of physical diseases and the healing of systemic racism.
- casting demons out of one person and casting demons out of corrupt and oppressive systems.
- conversion of one person to Christ and conversion of entire Christian denominations from heretical apartheid.
- uninhibited joy of free ecstasy in the Spirit and the unrestrained joy of free obedience in a life of holiness.
- willing reception of all sign gifts of the Spirit and the willing growth of all fruit of the Spirit.

The presence of the kingdom here and now is evidenced in signs of the future kingdom. The vision of that future hope of Revelation 21 when there will be no more sickness, pain, crying, or death can be experienced in part here and now because the kingdom has come even though it is not yet complete. This is why we pray and preach, serve and teach, evangelize and praise. This is why we declare today with Jesus: "The kingdom of God has come upon you" (Matt. 12:28).

TESTIMONIES FROM . . .

ARISTIDES (A CHRISTIAN PHILOSOPHER, A.D. 125)
They walk in all humility and kindness, and falsehood is not found among them. They love one another. They despise not the widow, and grieve not the orphan. Whoever has distributes liberally to whoever has not. If they see a stranger, they bring him under their roof, and rejoice over him as if he were their own brother; for they call themselves brothers, not after the flesh, but after the Spirit of God. When one of their poor passes away from the world, and any of them see him, then he provides for his burial according to his ability; and if they hear that any of their number is imprisoned or oppressed for the name of their Messiah, all of them provide for his needs and if it is possible that he may be delivered, they deliver him. And if there is among them a man that is poor and needy, and they have not an abundance of necessities, they fast two or three days that they may supply the needy with their necessary food.
—Howard Snyder, *A Kingdom Manifesto*, InterVarsity Press, 1985, p.80.

BRITISH GREAT AWAKENING (1730)

Actually, the most powerful demonstration of the Messianic kingdom we have yet seen may be the impact of the Wesleyan phase of the Great Awakening on the British Empire. . . . A single Anglican parish in Clapham, near London, contributed business leaders and the parliamentarian William Wilberforce, who could reach the levers of power in the Empire. While modern laity may feel they are doing well to keep their own spiritual sanity and reach a few of their peers in personal evangelism, the Clapham laity set out to change the face of England. They attacked moral corruption until the dissolute Regency period yielded to the Victorian era. They lived out an evangelical theology of liberation, moving beyond the redemption of individual souls to bring about the abolition of the slave trade and the release of slaves with the Empire (at a cost of 20,000,000 pounds to the British Treasury), deliverance from wage slavery on the home front and the conversion of the British Empire from an instrument of colonial exploitation into a rail system for the delivery of the gospel. Their successors attacked the abuses of the Industrial Revolution until child labor was abolished and public school for commoners became a reality. No clearly articulated theology of the kingdom of God motivated this great surge of spiritual and social transformation. But its cutting edge was a laity detached from the struggle for success or survival in the kingdom of self and committed to establishing the reign of Christ through their vocations.

—Richard Lovelace, *Renewal as a Way of Life*, InterVarsity Press, 1985, p. 55.

KEN BLUE (1987)

A group of friends and I spent two hours praying over three people in wheelchairs one evening after a healing seminar [in Vancouver, British Columbia]. One of the three was a woman in the final stages of multiple sclerosis, another was a man with a spinal injury which left him paralyzed from the chest down, and the third was an ex-dancer who now could not even stand upright because of severe arthritis. We prayed with the same love and skill or lack of them for all three, yet at the end of two hours only one was up and walking—the lady with MS. She seemed to have no more faith than the others and claimed to be no more deserving; yet after two years in her chair she got up. Months later and still improving, she is now almost back to normal. The remaining two are grateful for the loving care they received then and since, but are only slightly improved physically. . . . What, might we ask, is the significance of a few healings and deliverances in a world so thoroughly broken and diseased? These parables (Matthew 13) teach that what seems insignificant today will be fully established tomorrow. Our healings now seem small in light of the enormous need, but these healings are genuine manifestations of the new world coming. The kingdom of God has come among us; we may participate in it now, even in its incompleteness, looking forward to the day of its consummation at the return of Christ.

—*Authority to Heal,* InterVarsity Press, 1987, p. 111.

REFORMED REFLECTIONS

THE HEIDELBERG CATECHISM, Q&A 123
Q. What does the second request mean?

A. *Your kingdom come* means,
   Rule us by your Word and Spirit in such a way
     that more and more we submit to you.

   Keep your church strong, and add to it.

Destroy the devil's work;
destroy every force which revolts against you
and every conspiracy against your Word.

Do this until your kingdom is so complete and perfect
that in it you are
all in all.

> This answer is written as a prayer. Reflect on how God's
> answer would change your life, your family, your church,
> your city, your nation, our world.

**OUR WORLD BELONGS TO GOD: A CONTEMPORARY TESTIMONY,
STANZA 2**
From the beginning,
Through all the crises of our times,
Until his kingdom fully comes,
God keeps covenant forever.
God is King! Let the earth be glad!
Christ is Victor; his rule has begun. Hallelujah!
The Spirit is at work, renewing the creation.
Praise the Lord!

> Reflect on how you have witnessed the presence
> of God's kingdom and Jesus' lordship.

QUESTIONS TO THINK ABOUT
▸ What is a good definition of the kingdom of God?
▸ Is the kingdom the same as the church?
▸ What is the kingdom? Where is it? When is it? Who is in it?
▸ Think of some ways the kingdom of God is established today.
▸ What are some signs of the kingdom that you see?

PRAYER AND PRACTICE

Pray the Lord's Prayer every day this week as part of your devotions.

Watch for specific signs of the coming of the kingdom here and now "on earth as it is in heaven." Pray that the Lord will help you recognize these signs when they happen and to use you to make them happen.

ADDITIONAL RESOURCES

BOOKS

▸ Bright, John. *The Kingdom of God.* New York: Abingdon Press, 1953.
▸ Ridderbos, Herman. *The Coming of the Kingdom,* translated by H. deJongste. Philadelphia: The Presbyterian and Reformed Publishing Co., 1975.
▸ Williams, Don. *Signs, Wonders and the Kingdom of God.* Ann Arbor, Mich.: Servant Publications, 1989.
▸ Wimber, John, with Kevin Springer. *Power Evangelism.* San Francisco: Harper and Row, 1986.

CHAPTER SIX

DEMONSTRATING THE POWER OF THE HOLY SPIRIT

For your gift of God the Spirit,
power to make our lives anew,
pledge of life and hope of glory,
Savior, we would worship you.
Crowning gift of resurrection
sent from your ascended throne,
fullness of the very Godhead,
come to make your life our own.

He, the mighty God, indwells us;
his to strengthen, help, empower;
his to overcome the tempter—
ours to call in danger's hour.
In his strength we dare to battle
all the raging hosts of sin,
and by him alone we conquer
foes without and foes within.

Father, grant your Holy Spirit
in our hearts may rule today,
grieved not, quenched not, but unhindered,
work in us his sovereign way.
Fill us with your holy fullness,
God the Father, Spirit, Son;
in us, through us, then, forever,
shall your perfect will be done.

When I was growing up, my parents faithfully fulfilled their baptism vows and taught me to love and serve the Lord. They and my church helped disciple me, and when I was 17 I made public profession of faith in Jesus Christ as my Lord and Savior. I graduated from a Christian school, a Christian college, and seminary. But somehow I never really learned about the work and power of the Holy Spirit.

This section will focus on the need for Christians, having received the Holy Spirit in salvation, to be continually filled by the Holy Spirit and to receive all the gifts and fruit of the Spirit. Such filling puts Christians in a spiritual position to be used by God to demonstrate the power of the Spirit through signs and wonders today. To understand this third purpose of signs and wonders, we will examine

▸ the biblical revelation of the Holy Spirit.
▸ teachings about the Spirit's work throughout the history of the church.
▸ the impact of the Spirit's work in the lives of believers.

THE BIBLICAL REVELATION OF THE HOLY SPIRIT

THE HOLY SPIRIT IN THE OLD TESTAMENT
In the Old Testament the work of the Holy Spirit included

▸ being present in creation (Gen. 1:2).
▸ filling a person for a special task (Ex. 31:3; 1 Sam.10:6-10; Isa. 61:1; Ezek. 11:5-10).
▸ giving divine revelation (2 Sam. 23:2).

We also see that the Spirit is

▸ everywhere present (Ps. 139:7).
▸ poured out (Joel 2:28-29).
▸ powerful (Zech. 4:6).
▸ removable (Ps. 51:11).

THE HOLY SPIRIT IN THE NEW TESTAMENT

In the New Testament the Holy Spirit was involved in Jesus' miraculous conception and birth (Matt. 1:18). Jesus' ministry began with the Holy Spirit descending on him at baptism (Luke 3:21). Jesus used the words of Isaiah to testify:

> "The Spirit of the Lord is on me because he has anointed me to preach good news to the poor. He has sent me to proclaim freedom for the prisoners and recovery of sight for the blind, to release the oppressed, to proclaim the year of the Lord's favor."
> —Luke 4:18-19

Jesus promised the Spirit to the disciples (John 14:15-31) and after his resurrection breathed on them and said, "Receive the Holy Spirit" (John 20:22). We also see that the Spirit gives words to speak (Mark 12:36; 13:11).

▸ moves, directs, and leads (Luke 2:27; Acts 8:29; 16:7).
▸ gives joy (Luke 10:21).
▸ lives with us, counsels, teaches, reminds (John 14:16-17, 25-26).
▸ testifies about Jesus (John 15:26).
▸ convicts the world of sin and guides us into all truth (John 16:8, 13).
▸ brings glory to Jesus by taking from what is his and making it known to us (John 16:14).

These promises of the Spirit were fulfilled at Pentecost when the Spirit was poured out on all believers and the prophecy of Joel was fulfilled: "'In the last days, God says, I will pour out my Spirit on all people. . . . I will show wonders in the heaven above and signs on the earth below. . .'" (Acts 2:17,19). In the book of Acts, God did signs and wonders through the apostles and disciples to demonstrate the power of the Holy Spirit. Then and now, the Spirit

▸ comes on believers (Acts 1:8).
▸ fills believers (Acts 4:8; 9:17).
▸ intercedes for believers (Rom. 8:26-27).
▸ sanctifies believers (Rom. 15:16).
▸ encourages the church (Acts 9:31).
▸ tells believers what to do (Acts 11:28).
▸ searches all things (1 Cor. 2:10).
▸ gives different gifts to each one (1 Cor. 12).

- gives testimony (1 Cor. 12:3).
- ignites faith and obedience (1 John 3:23-24).

GIFTS OF THE SPIRIT

We've noted that the Spirit gives gifts to all those who have received the Spirit. The primary Scriptures in the New Testament describing spiritual gifts are

- Romans 12:6-8
- 1 Corinthians 12:1-11
- Ephesians 4:11
- 1 Peter 4:10-11

Scripture clearly speaks of many different gifts that are given for the common good, emphasizing that not all receive every gift, but that all do receive at least one gift. Many different opinions exist about exactly how many spiritual gifts the Spirit gives. From the Scripture passages cited, one can count nineteen gifts:

- prophesying
- serving
- teaching
- encouraging
- contributing to the needs of others
- leadership
- showing mercy
- the message of wisdom
- the message of knowledge
- faith
- healing
- miraculous powers
- discernment of spirits
- speaking in tongues
- interpretation of tongues
- apostle
- evangelist
- pastor
- administration

I do not believe that the apostle Paul intended to give us a complete or closed listing of gifts the Spirit may give. Peter Wagner, in his book *Your Spiritual Gifts Can Help Your Church Grow* (Regal Books, pp. 262-263), also includes celibacy, voluntary poverty, martyrdom, hospitality, intercession, exorcism, and being a missionary.

The gifts of the Spirit that seem more "supernatural" are often called *sign* gifts. However, terms like *supernatural* and *sign* are somewhat misleading. All gifts of the Spirit are signs that point to Christ and are supernatural in character. In Scripture the sign gifts are not elevated above the others as proof of "receiving the Spirit." In fact, the gift of love is called the greatest (1 Cor. 13:13).

TEACHINGS ABOUT THE HOLY SPIRIT THROUGHOUT CHURCH HISTORY

Biblical interpretation related to spiritual gifts is strongly influenced by context, experience, and church history. Although the work of the Holy Spirit is included and emphasized in the Reformed confessions, the Reformation sparked a strong reaction against the theological and experiential abuses of that time. On the one hand, the Reformers reacted against Roman Catholic claims that miracles proved the truth of their doctrine. On the other hand, Anabaptist enthusiasts claimed that the gifts of the Spirit brought new revelation.

Only since the Reformation have the *sign* gifts been discouraged and spoken of as having ceased with the age of the apostles. This is what John Calvin taught, and this position was strongly reinforced in twentieth-century Reformed circles through B. B. Warfield's book *Counterfeit Miracles* (The Banner of Truth Trust, 1972), first published in 1918.

The Reformation brought about renewal in the life of the church through a return to the Scriptures and the doctrine of salvation by grace alone. The Reformed leaders emphasized personal piety and spiritual renewal and the work of the Holy Spirit in salvation and sanctification, but the emphasis on doctrinal soundness and intellectual orthodoxy was emphasized over the power of the Holy Spirit to fill us as witnesses and with gifts.

As the Wesleyan Holiness movement and the Great Awakening began in England and the United States in the eighteenth century, a renewed emphasis was placed on the work and power of the Holy Spirit. The twentieth-century Pentecostal movement, with its roots in these holiness and revival movements, fostered the teaching that the gift of tongues is evidence of receiving the Holy Spirit. Richard Lovelace, in his book *Dynamics of Spiritual Life* (InterVarsity Press, 1979, pp. 120-21), records this landmark:

> In 1900, the American Bible teacher Charles Parham concluded from study of the book of Acts that the initial evidence of an individual's reception of "the baptism of the Holy Spirit" should be the exercise of the gift of tongues. Shortly after this the gift began to be experienced among his students.

Little biblical foundation for this teaching exists, and it too arises more out of historical context than biblical truth. The gift of tongues or languages is evidenced only three times in Acts:

- at Pentecost (Acts 2:4).
- at the conversion of Cornelius (10:46).
- when followers of John the Baptist who had not even heard about the Holy Spirit were baptized in the name of Jesus (19:6).

Acts records many instances in which people are described as "spirit-filled" but they do not speak in tongues (4:8, 31; 8:39). We read other examples in Acts of people, including the apostle Paul (9:17-19), being saved and converted but not speaking in tongues (2:41; 4:4). Although speaking in tongues is clearly one of the gifts of the Spirit that continues to function, no biblical evidence exists to make it the gift that distinguishes those receiving the Spirit or to elevate it above other gifts. While affirming his use of this gift, Paul plays down its use in the congregational life of the church (1 Cor. 14).

Both the Reformation reaction to the sign gifts of the Spirit and the Pentecostal pronouncement that the gift of tongues confirms receiving the Spirit are examples of historical context dictating biblical interpretation. In 1973, the Christian Reformed Church recognized and affirmed that the sign gifts have not ended but neither is the gift of tongues the sole mark of receiving the Holy Spirit. Counsel to the churches included the following:

We urge the whole church, especially through her teaching and pastoral ministries, to renew her awareness of and desire for the gifts of the Spirit in accord with the Scriptures, "for the equipment of the saints, for the work of ministry, for building up the body of Christ, until we all attain to the unity of the faith and of the knowledge of the Son of God, to mature manhood, to the measure of the stature of the fulness of Christ (Eph 4:12-13). We call on the church to recognize the freedom of the Spirit to bestow his gifts according to his will, and that the Scriptures do not restrict the *charismata* spoken of by the apostolic witness to the apostolic age. Let the church be open to an acknowledgement of the full spectrum of the gifts of the Spirit.

—"Neo-Pentecostalism," *Acts of Synod 1973*, Christian Reformed Church in North America, 1973, p. 481.

Although the apostle Paul encourages us to "eagerly desire spiritual gifts" (1 Cor. 14:1), I must confess that I had not eagerly desired many of the gifts of the Spirit because I did not believe they still existed. Nor did I understand how they continued to function in the life of the church. Even as I write this, I still struggle to lead my congregation into a fuller use of all of the spiritual gifts. I recognize that my own fears and inhibitions have kept me from welcoming all of the spiritual gifts in my own life and from encouraging and activating others.

THE IMPACT OF THE SPIRIT'S WORK IN THE LIVES OF BELIEVERS

BAPTIZED WITH THE SPIRIT

Jesus' ministry began at his baptism when the Father spoke and the Spirit descended. Jesus' ability to do signs and wonders also began at this point in time. Although Pentecost marked the initial outpouring of the Holy Spirit on the church, the Spirit continued to be poured out in many ways.

Our use and practice of spiritual gifts is often closely related to our understanding of baptism in the Spirit. The phrase "baptism in/with the Holy Spirit" is only used four times in Scripture in

- Matthew 3:11 and parallel passages (Mark 1:8; Luke 3:16; John 1:33).
- Acts 1:5.
- Acts 11:16.
- 1 Corinthians 12:13.

This baptism has often been interpreted to be a second encounter with God that every Christian must have to equip him or her for service as experienced by the apostles, the followers of John the Baptist, and Cornelius (Acts 2:4; 10:46; 19:6). But the Scriptures also speak of those who received the Holy Spirit as a result of belief, without mentioning the term *baptism* (Acts 8:14-19; 9:17-18; 10:44-46; 19:1-6).

The 1973 Synodical Study Report of the Christian Reformed Church clarified the traditional Reformed perspective in affirming that believers receive the Holy Spirit when they are "born again of the Spirit of God." This rebirth has traditionally been called regeneration and begins our life-long conversion. The report also recognized the need for continued openness to the ongoing work of the Spirit.

> We urge the whole church, and every member, to live in close fellowship with the Lord Jesus Christ, and not to "quench" (1 Thess. 5:19) or "grieve" (Eph. 4:30) the Holy Spirit but to be "filled with the Spirit" (Eph. 5:18) and to "live" (Rom. 8:13), "walk" (Gal. 5:25), and "be led" (Rom. 8:14, Gal. 5:18) by the Spirit, according to the admonitions of the apostle Paul, so that the joy of salvation and the fruit of the Spirit may be ever more evident in their lives.
> —"Neo-Pentecostalism," *Acts of Synod 1973*, Christian Reformed Church in North America, 1973, p. 481.

Most misunderstandings about baptism in the Holy Spirit can be resolved through a biblical understanding of the work of the Holy Spirit. This includes the pre-regeneration work of the Spirit, resulting from the call of God himself, in igniting a flame of faith that will enable someone to believe. The apostle Peter told those who responded to the Word of God on the day of Pentecost to "repent and be baptized . . . and you will receive the gift of the Holy Spirit" (Acts 2:38). This is the indwelling of the Holy Spirit that is sometimes also referred to as the "baptism in the Holy Spirit." Still, having been called to faith by the Spirit and regenerated (born again) by the Spirit, we may or may not be "filled with the Spirit."

Many Christians are like the followers of John the Baptist in Acts 19 who "had not even heard that there is a Holy Spirit."

We are filled and refilled with the Spirit many times in different ways. What is needed is not just a second blessing of the Holy Spirit, but daily, hourly, momentary blessings of the Holy Spirit to live out a transformed Christian life.

FILLED WITH THE SPIRIT

Although receiving the Holy Spirit may be a once-and-for-all experience, being filled with the Spirit is not. This filling of the Spirit gave Jesus' followers

▸ boldness in the face of danger.
▸ unity among themselves.
▸ a willingness to share material goods.
▸ the ability to perform miraculous signs.

Although Christians receive the Holy Spirit when they believe, they need to be filled with the Spirit continually. Paul's call to the church to "be filled with the Spirit" (Eph. 5:18) is an imperative command in the present passive tense, meaning "let the Spirit continually fill you." We must continually be open to the filling of the Holy Spirit in order to experience the Spirit's power in our lives and receive and use all the gifts that the Spirit gives us.

In Reformed circles, an underemphasis on the work and power of the Holy Spirit has traditionally existed, along with a fear of any manifestations of the Holy Spirit that cannot be controlled or predicted. I have felt this fear personally and have discussed this fear with my church. As the Lord continues to teach me in this area, I am learning to give up my control and yield to the movement of the Holy Spirit. But I must confess I still find it hard.

Recognizing that we receive the Holy Spirit in salvation, we must pray for the filling or release of the Spirit. If we belong to Christ, his Spirit is in us. But having received the Holy Spirit does not mean that one has allowed the Holy Spirit complete control. We must pray for the filling of the Holy Spirit, for we cannot live a victorious Christian life without it.

The tension between baptism and fullness is clarified by understanding the different biblical uses of the word *filled*. The Old and New Testament refer to the Spirit *upon* and the Spirit *within*. In the Old Testament, the Holy Spirit came upon Balaam, Saul, and Samson with power, yet little godliness was evident in their lives. These acts of the Spirit could be considered a baptism in the Spirit. On the other hand, the Old Testament also refers to the work of the Holy Spirit within, giving a new heart and new spirit (Jer. 31:33; Ezek. 36:26).

In the New Testament, there are two Greek words for *filled*. The first is *pleitho*, which refers to the outer work of the Spirit, usually as a brief temporary filling. This is illustrated when Elizabeth, hearing Mary's greeting, "was filled with the Holy Spirit" (Luke 1:41) and when Zechariah was "filled with the Holy Spirit and prophesied" (v. 67) about the role his unborn son John would play. The second Greek work is *pleiroo*, which refers to the ongoing, inner work of the Holy Spirit. This can be illustrated by the qualifications the disciples established for deacons: "men from among you who are full of the Spirit and wisdom" (Acts 6:3). In Acts 11:24, Barnabas is described as "a good man, full of the Holy Spirit and of faith. . . ." This is the same word Paul uses in Ephesians 5:18: "Do not get drunk on wine [which just gives a passing high]. Instead, be filled with the Spirit."

As we have already seen, the grammar in these passages testifies to the ongoing consistent action of the Spirit's filling. Zeb Bradford Long of Presbyterian-Reformed Ministries International helped me understand this and explains it better than I can:

> God wants us to be filled with the Spirit in two distinct senses of the word. He wants us, on the one hand, to be open to all the inner workings of the Spirit in our character, preparing us for eternity and yielding the fruit of the Spirit, especially love. On the other hand, he wants us to be open to occasions when we can minister in his power through the gifts of the Spirit. . . . In the first instance, we "have" the Holy Spirit. He is described as being "in" us to change our character. Christian character arises from the slow, percolating work of the Holy Spirit. . . . In the second instance, the Holy Spirit "has" us. He chooses to use us in a moment to accomplish a ministry by his power. . . . This kind of power for service comes and goes. . . . The Christian church is not divided into congregations that "have" or "have not" the power of God. God's empowerment for ministry in a Christians' life is episodic, not permanent. . . . Too many Christians are content to be only half-filled with the Holy Spirit.

They are "filled" (pleitho) but not "filled" (pleiroo), having "the Spirit upon" but not "the Spirit within," or visa-versa.

—Zeb Bradford Long and Douglas McMurry, *Receiving the Power: Preparing the Way for the Holy Spirit,* Chosen Books, 1996, p. 87.

EMPOWERED BY THE SPIRIT

The Holy Spirit brings power to believers. The New Testament Greek word for *power (dunamis)* can also be translated as *miracle.* It is also used in relation to the proclamation of the Word and the kingdom of God (1 Cor. 4:20) and in relationship to the Holy Spirit and believers. Jesus promised his disciples, "You will receive power when the Holy Spirit comes on you" (Acts 1:8). The power the Spirit gives believers equips them for ministry and to be witnesses. Evidences of that Spirit-given power, including signs and wonders, are found throughout the rest of the New Testament.

This biblical balance recognizes the fullness of the Holy Spirit in gifts and fruit, in power and love. It accounts for exceptional outpourings of the Spirit and times of emptiness when we're in need of refilling. It accounts for the dramatic experiences with the Holy Spirit that may or may not have long-term effects. Once again, Long and McMurry (p. 88) offer a helpful image:

> The power gifts of the Holy Spirit are like ornaments on a Christmas tree. They are given from outside. They can be put on and pulled off and rearranged. The inward fruit of the Spirit is more like the fruit of a fruit tree. It grows gradually and comes not from the outside but through the life of the tree itself . . . in the mature Christian life, both the inner and outer operations of the Spirit are to be in balance.

One of my favorite parts of teaching the Alpha program in our church is the Holy Spirit weekend. We tackle these questions:

▸ Who is the Holy Spirit?
▸ What does the Holy Spirit do?
▸ How can I be filled with the Holy Spirit?

As part of our weekend, we always have a huge bonfire at the retreat center where we meet. What begins with one match rises up to be a fire leaping 30 feet into the sky. It is a beautiful image of the consuming fire of the Holy Spirit that brings warmth and light and change in our lives.

In this chapter we have seen that the work and power of the Holy Spirit are vital to our being Christ's witnesses, able to do what Jesus did. We must not just *get* filled—we must *stay* filled in order to minister in power and through signs and wonders.

Our relationship with Christ is lived out by the Holy Spirit living in us. This requires a life of faithful discipleship to not only do what Jesus did in signs and wonders but to do what Jesus did in practicing the spiritual disciplines that nurtured his relationship with the Father. Without true discipleship, any Christian will become weak and ineffective.

TESTIMONIES FROM . . .

IRENAEUS (A.D. 200)

Those who are in truth his disciples, receiving grace from him, do in his name perform (miracles), so as to promote the welfare of other men, according to the gift which each one has received from him. For some do certainly and truly drive out devils, so that those who have thus been cleansed from evil spirits both believe (in Christ), and join themselves to the Church. Others have foreknowledge of things to come; they see visions, and utter prophecies. Others still, heal the sick by laying their hands upon them, and they are made whole. Yea, moreover, as I have said, the dead even have been raised up and remain among us for many years. And what shall I more say? It is not possible to name the number of the gifts which the Church through the whole world has received from God in the name of Jesus Christ . . . and which she exerts day by day for the benefit of Gentiles.

—David F. W. Wells, *God the Evangelist,*
William B. Eerdmans Publishing Co., 1987.

A. W. TOZER (1969)

In my sober judgment the relation of the Spirit to the believer is the most vital question the church faces today. . . . Before you can be filled with the Spirit you must desire to be filled. Are you sure that you want to be possessed by a Spirit other than your own? That Spirit, if he ever possesses you, will be the Lord of your life! Do you want to hand the keys of your soul over to the Holy Spirit? Again, are you sure that you need to be filled? Can't you get along the way you are?. . . If you feel that there are levels of spirituality, mystic deeps and heights of spiritual communion, purity and power that you have never known, that there is fruit which you know you should bear and do not, victory which you know you should have and have not—I would say, "Come on" because God has something for you. . . . Here is how to receive. First, present your body to him (Rom. 12:1-2). God can't fill what he can't have. . . . The second thing is to ask (Luke 11:9-11). . . . He chooses to have us ask; so why not ask? Acts 5:32 tells us the third thing. God gives his Holy Spirit to them that obey him. The next thing is, have faith (Gal. 2:20). We receive him by faith as we receive the Lord in salvation by faith. He comes as a gift of God to us in power.

—*Gems from Tozer: Selections from the Writings of A. W. Tozer.* Send the Light Trust, 1969, pp. 13-14.

DAVID BEELEN (1987)

Let me tell you my story as a testimony that might enable more understanding of tongues in our congregation. Back in 1983, I was involved in a prayer group which got together every week and called upon the Lord to heal people. Sometimes when those persons came we formed a circle of love around them, touching them lightly and then very calmly and without making demands on God, interceded for the suffering person to find relief from his pain. Sometimes people were healed and other times they were not. One man kept coming back. He had chronic headaches for years, and they had even kept him from steady employment. He had suffered so long. We prayed and prayed for him; I in English and others in tongues and in English. One day as I struggled to pray sensitively yet another time for this man, I was impressed by the Holy Spirit that God wanted to show love to him. But there was something blocking that flow of love. I did not know how to pray. I did not have the courage to ask him what might be blocking Jesus' love to him. So I prayed silently. And I remember concentrating on my Lord and sensing his love for me and everyone in the room. Then I began to pray, silently in a tongue. And I prayed for a long time. No one in the room sensed any change, and I did not seem changed. I was the same person. The tongue did not "get out of control" or make me more emotional. I just felt a greater ability to be a pastor to people, to pray for them in the guidance and direction of the Holy Spirit. This taught me some things about the gift of tongues and how God might give this gift to others:

- ▶ My experience is not the pattern for everybody. God may use thousands of ways and means to give his gifts to his people.
- ▶ I had resolved in myself that I desired the gift of tongues but was content to allow God to decide the time.
- ▶ I had lost any fear I had that tongues would turn me into someone that I did not like.
- ▶ I spent time praying with others who prayed or spoke in tongues and began to feel comfortable praying in their presence.
- ▶ I was part of a body of people who did not consider it a sign of spiritual maturity to speak in tongues. They fully accepted me even though I did not have this gift.
- ▶ I was involved in ministry and had a need of gifts to carry out that ministry with more power and freedom.

—David Beelen, *The Squarismatic Church.*
Grand Rapids: Madison Square Church, 1987, p. 18.

REFORMED REFLECTIONS

NICENE CREED
> . . . And we believe in the Holy Spirit, the Lord, the giver of life.
> He proceeds from the Father and the Son,
> And with the Father and the Son is worshiped and glorified.
> He spoke through the prophets. . . .

Reflect on what you've been taught about the Holy Spirit and how it influences your openness to the Spirit's working in your life.

OUR WORLD BELONGS TO GOD: A CONTEMPORARY TESTIMONY, STANZA 33
> The Spirit's gifts are here to stay
> in rich variety—
> fitting responses to timely needs.
> We thankfully see each other
> as gifted members of the fellowship
> which delights in the creative Spirit's work.
> He gives more than enough
> to each believer
> for God's praise and our neighbor's welfare.

Reflect on how you have received and are using power from the Holy Spirit to be a witness for Christ.

THE HEIDELBERG CATECHISM, Q&A 116
> **Q. Why do Christians need to pray?**
> A. Because prayer is the most important part
> of the thankfulness God requires of us.
> And also because God gives his grace and Holy Spirit
> only to those who pray continually and groan inwardly,
> asking God for these gifts
> and thanking him for them.

> Reflect on how you can pray continually and groan inwardly as you ask God for the Spirit's gifts.

QUESTIONS TO THINK ABOUT

▸ What do you think the disciples prayed about in Acts 1:14 as they were "constantly in prayer" for ten days between Jesus' ascension and Pentecost?

▸ What gifts of the Spirit do you see functioning in the life of your church?

▸ What are some of your spiritual gifts? How are you using them?

▸ Are you "eagerly desiring spiritual gifts" as Paul advises in 1 Corinthians 14? What gifts do you desire?

▸ What are some practical things you can do to stay filled with the Spirit?

▸ In what ways do we stifle the work and power of the Holy Spirit in our lives?

PRAYER AND PRACTICE

Pray aloud Paul's prayer for the Ephesians and make it personal.

I kneel before the Father, from whom his whole family in heaven and on earth derives its name. I pray that out of his glorious riches he may strengthen you with power through his Spirit in your inner being, so that Christ may dwell in your hearts through faith. And I pray that you, being rooted and established in love, may have power, together with all the saints, to grasp how wide and long and high and deep is the love of Christ, and to know this love that surpasses knowledge—that you may be filled to the measure of all the fullness of God. Now to him who is able to do immeasurably more than all we ask or imagine, according to his power that is at work within us, to him be glory in the church and in Christ Jesus throughout all generations, for ever and ever! Amen.

—Ephesians 3:14-20

> Use your spiritual gifts in one specific way this week
> for building up the body of Christ.

ADDITIONAL RESOURCES

BOOKS

▸ Long, Zeb Bradford and Douglas McMurry. *Receiving the Power: Preparing the Way for the Holy Spirit.* Grand Rapids, Mich.: Chosen Books, 1996.

▸ Stott, John R. W. *The Baptism and Fullness of the Holy Spirit.* Downers Grove, Ill.: InterVarsity Press, 1964.

CHAPTER SEVEN

TESTIFYING TO THE POWER OF PRAYER

PRAYER IS THE SOUL'S SINCERE DESIRE,
UNUTTERED OR EXPRESSED,
THE MOTION OF A HIDDEN FIRE
THAT TREMBLES IN THE BREAST.
PRAYER IS THE CHRISTIAN'S VITAL BREATH,
THE CHRISTIAN'S NATIVE AIR,
HIS WATCHWORD AT THE GATES OF DEATH;
HE ENTERS HEAVEN WITH PRAYER.
O THOU BY WHOM WE COME TO GOD,
THE LIFE, THE TRUTH, THE WAY,
THE PATH OF PRAYER THYSELF HAST TROD:
LORD, TEACH US HOW TO PRAY.

—William H. Havergal, 1846

Recently Jon DeBruyn, my good friend from seminary days, took a six-month sabbatical to travel the world asking this question: "What does a praying church look like, and how would you know one if you were in one?" One of the answers he found was that praying churches pray with passion. To illustrate praying with passion, Jon refers to Jesus' story of the friend at midnight (Luke 11:5-8). It was not the friendship or even the man's persistence that prompted his friend to open the door at midnight. It was the man's passionate pleas that got a response. The NIV translates this passion as *boldness* and the TNIV as *shameless audacity*. Jesus is teaching us that we can shake the gates of heaven with boldness and shameless audacity.

When I went on a prayer mission with Jon to Guatemala and Honduras this past summer, we did just that. As we stood on the mountain overlooking the city of Tegucigalpa, we could ask, "What difference can eight North Americans make by praying over a city of one million?" But by faith, we prayed in obedience and expectation, heeding Jesus' promise: "Ask and it will be given to you; seek and you will find; knock and the door will be opened to you" (Luke 11:9). So we prayed for deliverance from poverty and corruption, for good crops and enough jobs, for God's blessing on the children and families we could see far below, for the Spirit's empowering of the church as the body of Christ in the midst of the city. We prayed with passion—with shameless audacity—trusting in the promises of God.

The power of God manifested in signs and wonders is closely related to the power of prayer. In both the Old and New Testaments, many of the signs and wonders that God did were in response to the prayers of God's people. This chapter will explore how signs and wonders testify to the power of prayer. We will discuss

▸ the power of prayer as revealed in the Old and New Testaments.
▸ what Scripture teaches us about how and what to pray.
▸ the effects of prayer in our lives today.

The Power of Prayer
Revealed in Scripture

IN THE OLD TESTAMENT

The Bible tells of many times when God responded to his people's prayers with signs and wonders. Here are just a few examples:

- The sun stood still as a result of Joshua's prayer (Josh. 10:13).
- 185,000 Assyrians were slaughtered by an angel when King Hezekiah prayed (2 Kings 19).
- Hezekiah was healed of a terminal illness and given fifteen more years of life (2 Kings 20).
- When Solomon prayed at the dedication of the temple, "fire came down from heaven and consumed the burnt offering and the sacrifices" (2 Chron. 7:1).

God spoke to Solomon in response to his prayer and challenged his people to be steadfast in prayer if they expected him to hear and respond (2 Chron. 7:14). When God's people pray, God acts on their behalf. When they do not pray or are disobedient, God often refrains from acting and demonstrating his power (Ps. 34:16).

IN THE NEW TESTAMENT

In the book of Acts there are many examples of signs and wonders that God does in response to the prayers of his people. The disciples wait and pray for the Spirit to come (Acts 1:14). The promised outpouring of the Holy Spirit was a miraculous demonstration that Peter recognized as the fulfillment of Joel's prophecy (Acts 2). Later the disciples prayed, "Stretch out your hand to heal and perform miraculous signs and wonders through the name of your holy servant Jesus" (4:30). Following this prayer, the room shook and "they were all filled with the Holy Spirit and spoke the Word of God boldly" (4:31). In addition, the believers

- "were one in heart and mind" and "shared everything they had" (4:32).
- "with great power . . . continued to testify to the resurrection of the Lord Jesus" (4:33).

Peter was miraculously released from prison as the church fervently prayed for him (12:5-7), and the first missionary journey arose from a prayer meeting (13:1-3). Along with the signs and wonders that God gave in answer to prayer, we see the continued growth of the church in numbers and in discipleship.

In James, believers are encouraged to call on the elders to pray for the sick. They are promised that "the prayer offered in faith will make the sick person well. . . . The prayer of a righteous man is powerful and effective" (James 5:15-16).

Not all prayer results in signs and wonders. The Scriptures also describe believers who are

▸ "wrestling in prayer" (Col. 4:12).
▸ "patient in affliction, faithful in prayer" (Rom.12:12).
▸ "[continuing] night and day to pray and to ask God for help" (1 Tim. 5:5).

When Paul prayed for the removal of his thorn in the flesh, God answered in a different way than Paul anticipated. Three times Paul pleaded with God, but God said, "My grace is sufficient for you, for my power is made perfect in weakness" (2 Cor. 12:7-9). These verses help remind us of God's sovereignty, and they encourage us to keep praying even when we don't understand what God is doing.

TEACH US TO PRAY

In the New Testament, Jesus' disciples ask, "Lord, teach us to pray" (Luke 11:1). Jesus taught them what is known as the Lord's Prayer (vv. 2-4). We too can learn from Scripture how to pray and what to pray.

PRINCIPLES OF PRAYER
Several principles for effective prayer emerge from Scripture. God wants us to pray

▸ humbly (2 Chron. 7:14).
▸ as God wills (Matt. 26:39).
▸ boldly and persistently (Luke 11:5-8).
▸ confidently (Heb. 4:16).

- specifically (John 16:23-26).
- in Jesus' name (John 16:26).
- with the Holy Spirit's help (Rom. 8:26-27).
- continually (Eph. 6:18; 1 Thess. 5:17).
- with thanksgiving (Phil. 4:6).
- in repentance (James 5:16).
- obediently (1 John 3:22).

PRAYER IN ACCORD WITH THE WILL OF GOD

Let's look a bit more closely at the principle of praying as God wills. The biblical texts at the heart of what is often called the "name it and claim it" movement call us to expectant prayer. Jesus promises: "I will do whatever you ask in my name, so that the Son may bring glory to the Father" (John 14:13). Notice the two conditions Jesus establishes for prayer: (1) we are to pray in Jesus' name, and (2) we are to pray for things that will bring glory to God.

Such prayers can only be in complete accord with the will of God as revealed to us by the Word and Spirit. Jesus did not mean that God will grant every momentary whim we bring to him in prayer.

On the other hand, praying in accord with the will of God is often misunderstood based on Jesus' prayer in the Garden of Gethsemane: "My Father, if it is possible, may this cup be taken from me. Yet not as I will, but as you will" (Matt. 26:39). This prayer was an affirmation that Jesus was submitting his will to his heavenly Father; Jesus knew without a doubt that it was the Father's will for him to suffer and die on the cross. Jesus is expressing his human fear and aversion to crucifixion, but he submits that human fear to the revealed will of his Father.

We know that it is God's will for us to love our neighbors, forgive those who wrong us, evangelize those who are lost, and care for the needy. Even though we may not feel like doing these things, when we pray "Your will be done" we are radically aligning our rebellious human will with our Father's perfect will.

Many aspects of God's will are revealed to us through the Scriptures and by the Spirit. Scripture teaches that it is the will of God for the married to stay married, the hungry to eat, the naked to be clothed, the imprisoned to be released, the gossipers to be quiet, the demon possessed to be delivered, the rich to share, and so on. In many areas of our lives God is very clear about his will so that we can pray with authority, persistence, and confidence.

Although the will of God in the above areas may be clear, much debate has taken place about God's will in other areas, such as physical healing. But just as we can pray for the salvation of all sinners even though we know not all will be saved, we can pray for physical healing in all circumstances even though we know from experience that not all people will be healed.

This trust in the sovereignty and providence of God is summarized well in Article 13 of the Belgic Confession:

> We believe that this good God,
>   after he created all things,
> did not abandon them to chance or fortune
> but leads and governs them
>   according to his holy will
> in such a way that nothing happens in this world
> without his orderly arrangement. . . .
>
> This doctrine gives us unspeakable comfort
> since it teaches us
> that nothing can happen to us by chance
> but only by the arrangement of our gracious
> heavenly Father.
> He watches over us with fatherly care,
> keeping all creatures under his control,
> so that not one of the hairs on our heads
> (for they are all numbered)
> nor even a little bird
> can fall to the ground
> without the will of our Father.
>
> In this thought we rest,
> knowing that he holds in check
> the devils and all our enemies,
>   who cannot hurt us
>   without his permission and will.

Even when we don't understand, when we're overcome with grief, when God is silent, we still pray, trusting God's goodness.

BIBLICAL PRAYERS

We can learn much about prayer from the prayers of the saints that are recorded for us in Scripture. We find prayers of praise, confession, intercession, lamentation, thanksgiving—and combinations of all of these.

The prayer songs of Moses and Miriam in Exodus 15 praise God for the mighty ways that he delivered and provided for his people. David's prayer in 1 Chronicles 17 recalls God's past favor on the people of Israel and pleads for God's continuing blessing. Nehemiah's prayer of confession gives reason for God's dramatic judgment on his people and acknowledges God as the redeemer who keeps his promises (Neh. 1:5-11).

Daniel's prayer holds God accountable to the promises God made to hear, answer, and deliver (Dan. 9). Some prayers seem to put God to the test (Judg. 6) and challenge him to save face (2 Kings 19:15-19). Requests and petitions of intercession include deliverance from infertility (1 Sam. 1:11), from impossible situations (2 Kings 19:19), from prophetic proclamations (2 Kings 20:1-3), and from death (Jon. 2). These prayers remind us that God is able to do "immeasurably more than all we ask or imagine . . ." (Eph. 3:20).

Prayers are made in boldness, in God's will, and in expectation. Prayers frequently result in extraordinary responses (miracles) by God to situations of need or deliverance, works (wonders) that cause one to step back in awe at God's power, and responses (signs) that point to God's rule, sovereignty, and dominion.

Praying the Scripture is a good exercise in discipleship. Routinely, as part of your devotional time, pray aloud one or more of these Scripture prayers as spoken by

- Moses in Exodus 15:1-18.
- Gideon in Judges 6:36-40.
- Hannah in 1 Samuel 1:11; 2:1-10.
- Solomon in 1 Kings 8:22-62.
- David in 1 Chronicles 17:16-27.
- Hezekiah in 2 Kings 19:15-19; 20:2-3.
- Daniel in Daniel 9:4-19.
- Nehemiah in Nehemiah 1:5-11.
- Jonah in Jonah 2:1-9.
- Jesus in John 17.
- Paul in Ephesians 1:16-23; 3:14-21; Philippians 1:3-11; Colossians 1:9-13; 2 Thessalonians 1:11-12.

I frequently use the prayers of Paul listed above and pray them for our congregation. You'll note that I've included praying Scripture as part of the "Prayer and Practice" exercise at the end of each section in this book.

THE EFFECTS OF PRAYER IN OUR LIVES

THE POWER OF CORPORATE PRAYER

We have seen from the Scriptures that God always hears and answers sincere prayer, though not always in the way we expect. We have also seen that God's response to prayers can be in signs, wonders, and miracles as well as in other ways. This is especially true for our corporate prayer together as the Christian community.

Throughout church history, a close relationship between revival and prayer has been evident. For example, the Great Awakening of the eighteenth century was bathed in prayer that was rooted in a round-the-clock prayer meeting at Herrnhut that began in 1727 and continued for more than 100 years. This prayer foundation led to the beginning of the Protestant missionary movement. In 1999, a revival of the Herrnhut prayer began through the "24-7" prayer movement led by Pete Greig of England. To date, this movement has helped to establish thousands of "constant prayer" rooms in over 50 nations around the world.

As I write, our church is participating in a two-year process of church redevelopment with nine other churches. At a recent training, consultant Ken Priddy identified four habits of highly effective churches, the first of which was praying with power. Since prayer is one of the core values of our church, we have been trying to learn how to pray with power. This has resulted in a growing prayer ministry that includes a prayer shield for me, prayer warriors, prayer partners, prayer walkers, and a growing weekly prayer service.

PRAYER AND HEALING

A brief review of signs, wonders, and miracles of healing in the Bible identifies a variety of causes for sickness. At times sickness is a punishment for disobedience and sin (Ex. 32:35; 1 Cor. 11:27-30). Sometimes God is seen as the cause of sickness (Lam. 1:13). At other times, Satan is directly the cause (Job 1). At times, unconfessed sin can cause sickness

(Ps. 32). Other times sickness has nothing to do with one's personal sin (John 9:1-7). Not all sickness is healed (2 Cor. 12:7). Medicine is sometimes prescribed (1 Tim. 5:23). Sometimes people are healed as a result of their faith (Mark 10:52), sometimes when no faith is evident (John 5:1-15), and sometimes when healing is the result of the faith of one person praying for another (Matt. 17:20). Sometimes healing cannot take place because of lack of faith (Mark 6:5).

Praying for healing of illness and disease is not always simple. Often we decide what we think God can and cannot heal, and we pray accordingly. Sometimes we are afraid to pray for healing for fear of disappointing the person or ourselves if God does not heal immediately. Dr. Neil Plantinga, currently president of Calvin Seminary in Grand Rapids, Michigian, recognizes that we are often left with unanswered questions but that God is still in control.

> Every evil thing which comes into our lives must pass God's scrutiny, get through his filter, pass his screening test. None of it is out of his control. And all of it is turned, directed, redeemed so that good may be brought out of evil (Rom. 8:28). God averts all evil—or else turns it to our profit. . . . But we must not think that God authors, or originates, or causes sin. That is, in fact, a blasphemous idea.
> —*A Place to Stand,* Faith Alive Christian Resources, 1979, p. 63.

The Reformed perspective has always held these opposite truths in tension. God is sovereign over all things, yet God is not the author of evil. This is not a contradiction. They are both true. Yet we believe that God hears and answers our prayers—that prayer changes things. So we pray.

I learned this lesson many years ago as we prayed for Ruth. Ruth had been a Christian for all of her adult life. Living out her love for Christ in vibrant ways in her home, church, job, and neighborhood, she was loved and appreciated by all. At the age of 65, she was diagnosed with inoperable stomach cancer and given six months to live. Undeterred by this pronouncement, she requested the prayers of the church for healing, and together we continued steadfast in prayer. Near the predicted time of her death, another examination revealed that there were no signs of cancer remaining. The doctors called her the "miracle lady."

We rejoiced in God's healing mercy with Ruth, and she returned to work and other ministry involvements, thankful for each new day to live her life for the Lord. Then, four years later, cancer was again discovered.

She requested the prayers of the church again for healing and also underwent chemotherapy and radiation. Her condition grew worse. Her doctor told her not to expect another miracle. The elders laid hands on her and anointed her with oil in the name of the Lord. But the cancer spread.

On the night Ruth died, we had planned to celebrate the Lord's Supper with her and her husband around her bedside. Since her condition was worsening, we gathered to pray. As we stood in a circle around her bedside, Ruth tossed and turned in turmoil, calling on the name of the Lord, hardly aware of our presence. As we laid hands on her to pray, the Spirit revealed to all of us that it was not God's will to heal her physically but that God was going to take her to be with him. Our prayers changed from petition for healing to prayers of comfort and assurance in knowing Jesus and experiencing his presence in our midst. We had no sooner left Ruth's bedside than we received a call from her husband that she had gone home to be with Jesus. We were struck with a sense of awe and wonder at the might and mercy of God.

The laying on of hands and anointing with oil, both of which we used to minister to Ruth, have biblical precedent. In the Old Testament, oil was used to anoint a person for a special task in God's service, such as prophet, priest, or king. Oil was also used for medical reasons (Luke 10:34). In Mark 6:13, the disciples anoint with oil as a sign of the anointing of the Spirit and power of God related to healing. From these examples we can conclude that the use of oil has a legitimate place in the church today to remind us of the anointing of the Holy Spirit, to bring healing, and to consecrate for service.

In the same way, laying on of hands was used to convey authority and spiritual blessing as someone was commissioned for a specific ministry task (Acts 6:6; 13:3; 1 Tim. 4:14). This use is continued today in Christian Reformed churches when ordaining ministers, evangelists, elders, and deacons. Laying on of hands was also used when praying for new believers (Acts 8:19; 9:17; 19:6) and when praying for healing of the sick (Acts 28:8). Jesus and the disciples often touched people as they prayed for them and healed them. The hands of Christians represent the hands of Jesus as the body of Christ. Laying on of hands while praying for someone is a beautiful reminder of the Lord's personal touch and almighty power. We should joyfully exercise this biblical privilege when praying for one another.

PRAYER AND MISSION

Christ's authority is conveyed to Christians through his commissions to the church, his present lordship, and the empowerment of believers with the Holy Spirit. This authority puts Christians in a powerful position to carry out Christ's mission, but it is this very area of prayer that is often the weakest area.

Our congregation is learning how to prayer walk in our community. We have discovered that prayer walking is a wonderful way to witness for Christ and carry out his mission. Much like Jesus sent his first disciples out on their trial mission in Matthew 10, we go in groups of at least two to pray for people we meet, the neighborhoods we walk through, and the businesses we pass. The results?

▸ The pizza man stops making pizza for prayer.
▸ The cleaners stops pressing clothes for prayer.
▸ The shopkeepers stop for prayer.
▸ People we don't even know invite us into their homes for prayer.
▸ Gang members gather in a circle on their corner for prayer.
▸ Alcoholics put aside their bottles for prayer.

What we have experienced is that just about everyone wants prayer. It is a wonderful way to bring people who are far from God to the throne of grace for the salvation, healing, deliverance, protection, and hope that only God can give.

As a child, I had a small plaque on my bedroom wall that read: "Prayer changes things." Although I always knew this was true, I often didn't pray like it was true. In this chapter, we have seen that God responds to our prayers, and often responds with signs, wonders, and miracles. Individuals and congregations will pray with power by applying the principles of prayer to their prayer life. Doing this enables us to experience the power of God in ways that those who do not pray will not experience. So it is that we pray for conversions and healings, deliverance of bodies and minds, jobs and justice, freedom from addiction and from prison, an end to war and terror.

TESTIMONIES FROM . . .

FRANCIS OF ASSISI (A.D. 1200)

And when he had heard what they had to tell, St. Francis himself went to this perverse leper, and going up to him he saluted him, saying: "God give thee peace, my beloved brother!"

But the leper answered: "What peace can I have from God, who has taken away peace and all good from me and caused me to be covered with rottenness and to stink?"

And St. Francis said: "My son, have patience, for as much as the infirmities of the body are given by God in this world for the salvation of the soul, because they are of great merit when born patiently."

The sick man replied: "And how can I bear patiently the continual pain which afflicts me both day and night?"

. . . Then St. Francis, knowing by inspiration from God that this leper was possessed by the evil spirit, went and gave himself up to prayer and besought God devoutly for him. As his prayer ended, he returned to the leper, and said: "Now, I will serve thee myself, since thou art not contented with the other."

"As thou pleasest," said the man, "but what canst thou do for me more than the other?" And St. Francis answered him: "Whatever thou desirest, I will do."

Said the leper: "I desire that thou shouldst wash me all over, because my wounds smell so foully that I cannot bear with myself."

Then St. Francis quickly had water heated and many sweet smelling herbs put into it; and after this, he stripped the leper and began to wash him with his own hands whilst another Brother poured water. And by Divine miracle, wherever St. Francis touched him with his holy hands the leprosy departed and the flesh became perfectly whole; and as the flesh began to heal, so the soul began to be healed also. Wherefore the leper, seeing that he was on the way to be healed, began to have great compunction and repentance for his sins and to weep bitterly; so that as the body was cleansed outwardly from the leprosy by the washing with water, so the soul was purified inwardly from sin by repentance and by tears.

—The Little Flowers of St. Francis of Assisi,
Daughters of St. Paul, 1976, pp. 90-91.

GEORGE WHITEFIELD (1744)

Went out for the first after a long and dangerous relapse which threatened my life more than my late visitation at York. My pains were more acute and my weakness much more sensible. The help of another Physician was called in. Nothing was wanting that could be necessary. All were officious to attend upon and sit up with me, and above all the Dear Redeemer was pleased to give me his presence both to support and compose. Several times I seemed to be breathing my last, but I really believe the prayers of God's people brought me back. Some spent a whole night in that exercise, and others were insistent with God by day. O what am I! The Lord humble me, reward my friends, and for his Dear Son's sake grant that I may come out of this furnace like gold tried seven times in the fire, and that his people may not be disappointed of their hope. Even so, Lord, Jesus. Amen!

—*George Whitefields's Journals,* The Banner of Truth Trust, 1960 (1756), p. 525.

DAVID BRYANT (1970)

As a pastor in Kent, Ohio, in 1970, I was forced to God's threshold after witnessing the Kent State University shootings that fateful day in May. The trauma of that tragic incident not only sealed the mood of the country about Vietnam but, ultimately, the course of history and nations. Our church, as a body, felt convicted. The impact we were having on the world for Christ was negligible compared to the impact of the student-national guard confrontation on the KSU campus. By fall, five men in the church joined me in seeking some answers from God. We agreed to meet for six weeks of prayer, four nights a week, two hours a night. The first night we met, we sat there, staring at each other with half smiles as if to say, "Well, what do we do now?" None of us had ever prayed like this before. One suggested we pray through Scripture. That made sense. We chose Ephesians. And why not? Ephesians has six chapters, and we were committed to meet for six weeks. And what an unforgettable six weeks. You can't pray through Scripture like Ephesians and stay the same. Paul swept us along in God's purposes for the nations and the church. And I believe we saw some key evidences of spiritual awakening as a result.

—*Concerts of Prayer,* Regal Books, 1984, p. 22.

REFORMED REFLECTIONS

THE HEIDELBERG CATECHISM, Q&A 117

Q. How does God want us to pray so that he will listen to us?

A. First, we must pray from the heart
to no other than the one true God,
who has revealed himself in his Word,
asking for everything he has commanded us to ask for.
Second, we must acknowledge our need and misery,
hiding nothing,
and humble ourselves in his majestic presence.
Third, we must rest on this unshakable foundation:
even though we do not deserve it,
God will surely listen to our prayer
because of Christ our Lord.
That is what he promised us in his Word.

> Reflect on how much you believe that prayer changes things.

THE HEIDELBERG CATECHISM, Q&A 118

Q. What did God command us to pray for?

A. Everything we need, spiritually and physically,
as embraced in the prayer
Christ our Lord himself taught us.

> Reflect on why we are often quicker to call the doctor for a
> prescription than the elders for prayer.

THE HEIDELBERG CATECHISM, Q&A 120

Q. Why did Christ command us to call God "Our Father"?

A. At the very beginning of our prayer
Christ wants to kindle in us
what is basic to our prayer—
   the childlike awe and trust
   that God through Christ has become
our Father.
Our fathers do not refuse us
   the things of this life;
God our Father will even less refuse to give us
   what we ask in faith.

Reflect on what Heidelberg Catechism
Q&A 120 means for your prayer life.

QUESTIONS TO THINK ABOUT

▸ Why might you be quicker to pray for your spiritual needs than your physical needs?

▸ Are there some physical needs we should not ask God to meet? Why or why not?

▸ Why is it important that we ask in faith?

▸ How are you applying "the principles of prayer" in your prayer life?

▸ When might you pray prayers from Scripture as suggested in this chapter?

PRAYER AND PRACTICE

Pray aloud Nehemiah's prayer of corporate confession:
"O LORD, God of heaven,
the great and awesome God,
who keeps his covenant of love
with those who love him and obey his commands,
let your ear be attentive and your eyes open
to hear the prayer your servant is praying
before you day and night
for your servants, the people of Israel.

I confess the sin we Israelites,
including myself and my father's house,
have committed against you.
We have acted very wickedly toward you.
We have not obeyed the commands, decrees and laws
you gave your servant Moses. . . .
O LORD, let your ear be attentive to the prayer of
this your servant
and to the prayer of your servants who delight
in revering your name.
Give your servant success today
by granting him favor in the presence of this man."

—Nehemiah 1:5-7, 10

During the week ahead, practice personal
and/or corporate confession before the Lord.

ADDITIONAL RESOURCES

BOOKS

▸ Bryant, David. *Christ Is All.* New Providence: New Providence Publishers, 2004.

▸ Cymbala, Jim. *Breakthrough Prayer: The Secret of Receiving What You Need from God.* Grand Rapids, Mich.: Zondervan, 2003. (See also www.brooklyntabernacle.org.)

▸ Greig, Pete and Dave Roberts. *Red Moon Rising: How 24-7 Prayer Is Awakening a Generation.* Eastbourne, England: Relevant Books/ Kingsway Publications, 2005.

PERIODICAL

▸ *Pray—Encouraging a Passion for Christ Through Prayer* (bimonthly magazine published by Navigators. See also www.praymag.com.)

DVD

▸ *Prayer-walking: Taking Prayer to the Streets of Your City.* New York: New Hope. (See also www.praynewyork.com or www.newhope-newyork.com.)

ORGANIZATIONS/MOVEMENTS

Concerts of Prayer—Greater New York (www.copgny.org)

CHAPTER EIGHT

GIVING EVIDENCE OF OUR FAITH IN JESUS

WE'VE COME THIS FAR BY FAITH,
LEANING ON THE LORD,
TRUSTING IN HIS HOLY WORD—
HE'S NEVER FAILED US YET.
OH, CAN'T TURN AROUND,
WE'VE COME THIS FAR BY FAITH.
DON'T BE DISCOURAGED
WITH TROUBLE IN YOUR LIFE;
HE'LL BEAR YOUR BURDENS
AND REMOVE ALL MISERY AND STRIFE.

—Albert A. Goodson, 1965. © 1965, renewed 1993,
Manna Music, Inc. All rights reserved. Used by permission.

At Madison Avenue Church where I've served as pastor for over 27 years, we know the power of the gospel can break down the barriers of racism, prejudice, and separation to bring deliverance and reconciliation. "We've Come This Far by Faith" is one of our favorite songs. It testifies to the African-American struggle in our nation and in our congregation. It has been a theme song for as long as I've been at Madison Avenue.

Of the original six historic Christian Reformed churches founded in Paterson, New Jersey, Madison Avenue is the only one that remains. All the others moved to the suburbs, as did many churches throughout the nation. In the midst of the racial tensions of the 1960s, it took great faith for leaders of Madison Avenue to commit to staying in the city to minister. The multiracial character of our congregation is a result of the faith of our predecessors and a sign and wonder of God's kingdom.

This chapter will explore the relationship between our faith and God's response. We'll see how our sovereign God responds to our faith and how the signs and wonders that result give evidence of our faith. As we look at this fifth purpose of signs and wonders, we will

▸ define three kinds of faith.
▸ examine four ways faith and signs and wonders interrelate in Scripture.
▸ discuss the connection between faith and signs and wonders today.

DIFFERENT KINDS OF FAITH

The most well-known biblical definition of faith is in Hebrews 11:1: "Now faith is being sure of what we hope for and certain of what we do not see." In *A Greek-English Lexicon of the New Testament* (University of Chicago Press, 1957, p. 666) Walter Bauer says faith is "faith in the Divinity that lays special emphasis on trust in his power and his nearness to help, in addition to being convinced that he exists and that his revelations or disclosures are true."

While these are helpful definitions, let's look at three different ways faith is described in the Bible:

▸ faith by which we receive salvation
▸ faith to live a daily Christian life
▸ the gift of faith that is sometimes called "miraculous" faith

SAVING FAITH

When we receive salvation through faith, we enter into a relationship with God through Jesus Christ. Faith is the pipeline though which we receive the gift of grace. "For it is by grace you have been saved, through faith—and this not from yourselves, it is the gift of God—" (Eph. 2:8). Reformed thought has always stressed the work of the Holy Spirit in generating faith.

But we see the biblical paradox: we are called to believe, yet we cannot believe if the Spirit is not at work. We are elected to salvation and called to "believe in the Lord Jesus Christ, and you will be saved" (Acts 16:31). Yet what seems to be a contradiction is biblically true. The apostle Paul gives us a glimpse of that in Philippians 2:12-13: "Work out your salvation with fear and trembling, for it is God who works in you to will and to act according to his good purpose."

Reformed definitions of faith have stressed both knowledge and assurance as important elements of true faith. Faith is both knowing something in our heads and believing it with our hearts. John Calvin defined true faith as "a firm and certain knowledge of God's benevolence toward us, founded upon the truth of the freely given promise in Christ, both revealed to our minds and sealed upon our hearts through the Holy Spirit" (*Institutes of the Christian Religion*, The Westminster Press, 1960, p. 551).

The Heidelberg Catechism defines saving faith this way in Q&A 21:
True faith is
   not only a knowledge and conviction
      that everything God reveals in his Word is true;
it is also a deep-rooted assurance,
   created in me by the Holy Spirit through the gospel,
   that, out of sheer grace earned for us by Christ
      not only others, but I too,
      have had my sins forgiven,
      have been made forever right with God,
      and have been granted salvation.

FAITH TO LIVE THE CHRISTIAN LIFE

Recognizing our response of faith to the work of God in salvation is important as we look at the faith needed to live the Christian life. When Hebrews 11 recounts the heroes of faith, it focuses on what they did because they believed. Among those listed there are

▸ Noah, who built an ark when there was no water in sight (Gen. 6-8).
▸ Abraham, who moved from his home to a new land because God told him to (Gen. 12).
▸ the Israelites, who walked around the walls of Jericho seven times, following what seemed like a poor battle plan (Josh. 6).

For these heroes, faith involved obeying God's voice and direction in spite of the circumstances. This is the kind of faith that is lived out in the hard lessons of life and in obedience. This is the kind of faith that Jesus' disciples asked for more of when Jesus told them how many times they should forgive someone. This is the kind of faith that the apostle Paul calls the "shield of faith" (Eph. 6:16) that will defend us against all the attacks of the evil one.

The knowledge aspect of faith is important to make sure that our faith is in the true God and Father of our Lord Jesus Christ. Many people have faith in many things, but true faith is directed to God. The assurance aspect is also important because it is what enables Christians to go on believing in God in the midst of great adversity. This is the kind of faith Job expressed when, in the midst of all his loss and questions and pain, he could still confess: "I know that my Redeemer lives . . ." (Job 19:25). As the hymn writer says:

> I know not what of good or ill
> may be reserved for me,
> of weary ways or golden days,
> before his face I see.
> But "I know whom I have believed,
> and am persuaded that he is able
> to keep that which I've committed
> unto him against that day."
> —Daniel W. Whittle, 1883; based on 2 Timothy 1:12

But faith is more than just knowing and being assured—it is also acting. In James 2:17, we read that "faith by itself, if it is not accompanied by action, is dead." We respond obediently because we have faith. The story about Daniel's three friends is a good example. When King Nebuchadnezzar threatened to put Shadrach, Meshach, and Abednego in the fiery furnace if they didn't bow down to his idol, they responded in faith:

"The God we serve is able to save us from it, and he will rescue us from your hand, O king. But even if he does not, we want you to know, O king, that we will not serve your gods or worship the image of gold you have set up."

—Daniel 3:17-18

Daniel's friends recognized God's power to save them from the furnace, but they did not command God to deliver them. They recognized that the king couldn't do anything to them that would threaten their relationship with God. They had faith in all that God can do and faith to accept God's response to their situation.

We must know who God is and be persuaded by what God can do. Faith is not just something we know in our heads and are assured of in our hearts—it is also something that affects every decision and choice we make.

GIFTED FAITH

The Bible speaks of yet a third kind of faith. The apostle Paul identifies this faith in 1 Corinthians 12:9 as a spiritual gift and cautions, "If I have a faith that can move mountains, but have not love, I am nothing" (1 Cor. 13:2). Jesus described this faith as "small as a mustard seed" but able to move mountains (Matt. 17:20).

The 1973 Christian Reformed synodical report on Neo-Pentecostalism also recognized this spiritual gift of faith and described it thus:

This kind of faith may well be the kind of faith which trusts God to heal and perform miracles and may therefore be closely related to the other spiritual gifts. This faith should be distinguished from the faith by which alone a man is righteous before God (Rom. 1:16-17). Paul describes faith that is a spiritual gift as the kind of faith that removes mountains (1 Cor. 13:2; Matt. 7:20). Daniel's courage in the lion's den and Peter's act of walking on water may be examples of this kind of faith. As a spiritual gift, it cannot be expected that every believer has this kind of faith, though all may pray for it.

—*Acts of Synod 1973*, Christian Reformed Church in North America, 1973, p. 457.

Pastor and author Alvin J. Vander Griend includes the gift of faith as one of the "sign" gifts. In this context, faith is defined as "the special Spirit-given ability to know with certainty that God wills to do something and is certain to do it, in response to prayer, even when there is no concrete evidence" (Discover your Gifts and Learn How to Use Them (Student Manual), Faith Alive Christian Resources 1996, p. 91).

Dallas Willard describes this faith as "a significant, extra-human power over the evils of this present age and world, exercised both by individuals and by the collective church" (The Spirit of the Disciplines, InterVarsity Press, 1988, p. 42). Willard sees this faith as arising from Jesus' authority given to all disciples in the great commission (Matt. 28:18-20) and as something that can only be practiced when we are truly following Jesus as disciples. It is faith that arises out of our relationship with the risen Christ through the power of the Holy Spirit.

Reformed theologian Louis Berkhof called this "miraculous faith" and argued that it no longer existed. He, like John Calvin, saw miracles as part of God's special revelation prior to the completion of the canon of Scripture and ending with the age of the apostles. I respectfully challenge our Reformed fathers in this matter. In our study, we have seen that God continues to respond with signs and wonders as a result of the proclamation of the Word of God, the presence of the kingdom of God, the power of the Holy Spirit, and the power of prayer. Perhaps one reason why so few miracles have been experienced in Reformed churches is that we no longer expect them or believe God will do them.

FAITH AND SIGNS AND WONDERS IN SCRIPTURE

We see four ways faith and signs and wonders interrelate in Scripture. First, we note instances where a lack of faith prohibits or blocks signs and wonders:

▶ Jesus refuses to do miracles in Nazareth because of the peoples' lack of faith (Matt.13:58).
▶ Seeming to lose faith, Peter sinks into the water after taking his eyes off Jesus (14:30-31).
▶ Jesus attributes his disciples' inability to cast out a demon to a lack of faith and says, "I tell you the truth, if you have faith as small as a mustard seed, you can say to this mountain, 'Move from here to there' and it will move. Nothing will be impossible for you" (17:20-21).

Second, we see examples in the Bible when a person's faith leads to healing or to other signs and wonders:

▸ When a sick woman touched Jesus' coat and was healed, he said to her, "Your faith has healed you" (Mark 5:34).
▸ When Bartimaeus had his sight restored, Jesus said, "Your faith has healed you" (Mark 10:52).
▸ Paul healed a man who couldn't walk after he "saw that he had faith to be healed" (Acts 14:9).
▸ Paul commended the Galatians for their faith and the miracles God did as a result of it and asked, "Does God give you his Spirit and work miracles among you because you observe the law, or because you believe what you heard?" (Gal. 3:5).

It is important to observe that Jesus discerns and highlights the presence of faith in those seeking healing. Sometimes he even asks people if they have faith. After two men who were blind requested healing, Jesus responded, "According to your faith will it be done to you" (Matt. 9:29). Jesus also had compassion on those who did not have faith, such as the father of the demonized boy who prayed, "I do believe; help me overcome my unbelief!" (Mark 9:24).

Third, we find examples in Scripture where signs and wonders are done as a result of the faith of a person other than the person who is healed:

▸ Because a centurion demonstrated faith in Jesus, his servant was healed (Matt. 8:5-10). Jesus commented, "I have not found anyone in Israel with such great faith" (v. 10).
▸ Jesus healed a paralytic man when he saw the faith of the man's friends (Matt. 9:2).
▸ When Peter and John healed a man who begged at the gate of the temple, nothing is said about the man's faith, but the faith of the disciples is emphasized. "By faith in the name of Jesus, this man whom you see and know was made strong. It is Jesus' name and the faith that comes through him that has given this complete healing to him, as you can all see" (Acts 3:16).

Finally, we find examples in Scripture where signs and wonders are done even though no faith is evident:

- God provided manna in the wilderness for Israel, in spite of the fact that "they did not believe in God or trust in his deliverance" (Ps. 78:22).
- When Jesus raised a little girl from the dead, all those present, including his disciples, "were completely astonished" (Mark 5:42).
- When Jesus fed 5,000 people, no one, not even his disciples, expected or had faith that he could feed so many with five loaves and two fish. Andrew asked, "How far will they go among so many?" (John 6:9).
- Even when Jesus proceeded to raise Lazarus from the dead, Martha argued that the body would smell. Jesus responded, "Did I not tell you that if you believed, you would see the glory of God?" (John 11:40).

Miracles sometimes helped people to believe and come to a saving faith. Jesus exhorted his disciples to "believe me when I say that I am in the Father and the Father is in me; or at least believe on the evidence of the miracles themselves" (John 14:11). However, Jesus also recognized that many would witness miracles and still not believe (10:32; 15:24).

FAITH AND SIGNS
AND WONDERS TODAY

GOD'S PART AND OUR PART
When exploring the relationship between our faith and signs and wonders, especially since Jesus' resurrection, it is important to remember the purposes of signs and wonders. We've seen that signs and wonders

- proclaim the Word of God.
- demonstrate the presence of the kingdom of God.
- demonstrate the power of the Holy Spirit.
- testify to the power of prayer.
- give evidence of our faith in Jesus.
- defeat the devil.

Lack of faith in what God can do and low human expectations may limit God's response. When Peter marveled that the fig tree Jesus cursed had withered, Jesus says, "Have faith in God . . . whatever you ask for in prayer, believe that you have received it, and it will be yours" (Mark

11:22, 24). This exhortation to faith is repeated in John 14:12-14: "I tell you the truth, anyone who has faith in me will do what I have been doing." If we are to experience signs and wonders, faith in the power and might of God is vitally important.

Note that the emphasis is on God's part rather than ours. The term *faith healing* is usually used to refer to healing ministries that emphasize the faith of the person being healed as the *condition* for healing. Biblically, we see that healing is a gift of grace from God and that faith is not a tool to coerce God. A better phrase is *faith for healing*, meaning that we have faith in all that God can do while we trust God to do what is best for us.

Exactly how the gift of faith works in the midst of our lives may be a mystery that we cannot understand, but we must recognize that spiritual gifts, including the gift of faith, are given as needed to God's people in different situations for moments and seasons. Recognizing that faith is also a gift that God gives, let us "eagerly desire" it (1 Cor. 14:1).

CONFESSING OUR FAITH
Scripture calls us to confess out loud what we believe. The Psalms continually "sing" about the mighty acts of God and invite us to acclaim, "My mouth is filled with your praise, declaring your splendor all day long" (Ps. 71:8). Paul challenges us to publicly profess our faith in Jesus as our Lord and Savior, "for it is with your heart that you believe and are justified, and it is with your mouth that you confess and are saved" (Rom. 10:10).

At Madison Avenue Church, we recite the Apostles' Creed as a weekly confession of faith. As we prayer walk our communities, we declare out loud Jesus' lordship over the streets and homes and businesses we pass. Recently on one of the toughest corners of our neighborhood, we declared out loud a famous Abraham Kuyper quote: "There is not one square inch of the universe that is not under the lordship of Jesus Christ." We should not be ashamed to say what we believe; there is power in declaring it.

Faith recognizes the sovereign power of the living God who is the creator of the universe and shouts with the psalmist, "The Lord is King!" This faith is experienced in salvation, in daily Christian living, and through signs and wonders. This is faith that includes knowledge and assurance and also bold action, evidenced in what we believe God can and will do. This is the kind of faith that declares with the apostle Paul in Ephesians 3:20 that God is able "to do immeasurably more than all we ask or imagine, according to his power that is at work within us."

TESTIMONIES FROM . . .

MARTIN LUTHER (1516)

Night and day I pondered until I saw the connection between the justice of God and the statement that "the just shall live by his faith." Then I grasped that the justice of God is that righteousness by which through grace and sheer mercy God justifies us through faith. Thereupon I felt myself to be reborn and to have gone through open doors into paradise. The whole of Scripture took on a new meaning, and whereas before "the justice of God" had filled me with hate, now it became to me inexpressibly sweet in greater love. This passage of Paul became to me a gate to heaven. . . . If you have a true faith that Christ is your Savior, then at once you have a gracious God, for faith leads you in and opens up God's heart and will, that you should see pure grace and overflowing love.

—Roland H. Bainton, *Here I Stand: A Life of Martin Luther,* Mentor, 1950, p. 49.

CHARLES H. KRAFT (1989)

A bit of experience in praying for people, however, leaves one puzzled concerning just what part faith plays in the process. For a disturbing number of people with apparently very little faith seem to get immediately healed, while some with an apparently high faith level have not been healed! Recently a friend prayed for a man who agreed only reluctantly, stating "Nothing will happen." He was healed but didn't even notice it until two days later, yet his wife who seemed to have a lot of faith was left with her condition unhealed. People to whom I minister several times, however, seem to develop greater faith as time goes on.

—*Christianity with Power,* Servant Publications, 1989, p. 140).

MILLARD FULLER (1986)

I often meet with groups who are considering the formation of a new Habitat for Humanity project. One of the most frequently asked questions is, "How much money do we need to raise before we begin?" My answer is always the same: "A dollar. If you have less than a dollar, launching a project would be irresponsible." Then I explain that there is one other requirement. "You must also have a core group of committed people who are serious about serving the Lord using the economics of Jesus, and about helping his children find a decent place to live. If you have the dollar and the committed people, and you move on faith, the Lord will move with you." In fact, as Steve Anderson, of Chesapeake Habitat in Baltimore, frequently reminds us, "When you step out in faith and let the Lord lead, you have to run to keep up."

—*No More Shacks!*, Word Books, 1986, p.160.

REFORMED REFLECTIONS

THE BELGIC CONFESSION, ARTICLE 22

We believe that
for us to acquire the true knowledge of this great mystery
the Holy Spirit kindles in our hearts a true faith
that embraces Jesus Christ,
with all his merits,
and makes him its own,
and no longer looks for anything
apart from him. . . .

However,
we do not mean,
properly speaking,
that it is faith itself that justifies us—
for faith is only the instrument
by which we embrace Christ,
our righteousness.

But Jesus Christ is our righteousness
in making available to us all his merits
and all the holy works he has done
for us and in our place.
And faith is the instrument
that keeps us in communion with him
and with all his benefits.

When those benefits are made ours
they are more than enough to absolve us
of our sins.

> Reflect how faith helps keep you "in communion
> with [Jesus] and with all his benefits."

THE HEIDELBERG CATECHISM, Q&A 32
Q. But why are you called a Christian?
A. Because by faith I am a member of Christ
   and so I share in his anointing.
      I am anointed
      to confess his name,
      to present myself to him as a living sacrifice of thanks,
      to strive with a good conscience against sin and the devil
        in this life
   and afterward to reign with Christ
      over all creation
      for all eternity.

> Reflect on ways that you are by faith "a member
> of Christ and so . . . share in his anointing."

QUESTIONS TO THINK ABOUT
- Is taking medicine or going to a doctor after you've prayed for healing a sign of lack of faith? Explain your answer.
- As you think about the relationship between our faith and God's sovereignty, does faith make a difference in how God responds? Does faith assure the results we want? Does faith leave room for doubt? Give examples to support your answers.
- How can our faith help us to present ourselves "as a living sacrifice of thanks"?
- How does being a "member of Christ" help us to fight "against sin and the devil in this life"?

PRAYER AND PRACTICE
Pray aloud the prayer of Paul, Silas, and Timothy to the church of the Thessalonians:

> We constantly pray for you, that our God may count you worthy of his calling and that by his power he may fulfill every good purpose of yours and every act prompted by your faith. We pray this so that the name of our Lord Jesus may be glorified in you, and you in him, according to the grace of our God and the Lord Jesus Christ.
>
> —2 Thessalonians 1:11-12

Read James 5:13-16; then pray a prayer of faith this week for someone who is sick or in trouble.

ADDITIONAL RESOURCE

BOOK
- Cho, David Yonggi. *The Fourth Dimension,* Vol. 1. Gainsville: Bridge-Logos, 1979.

CHAPTER NINE

DEFEATING THE DEVIL

A MIGHTY FORTRESS IS OUR GOD,
A BULWARK NEVER FAILING;
OUR HELPER HE, AMID THE FLOOD
OF MORTAL ILLS PREVAILING.
FOR STILL OUR ANCIENT FOE
DOES SEEK TO WORK US WOE;
HIS CRAFT AND POWER ARE GREAT,
AND ARMED WITH CRUEL HATE,
ON EARTH IS NOT HIS EQUAL.

DID WE IN OUR OWN STRENGTH CONFIDE,
OUR STRIVING WOULD BE LOSING,
WERE NOT THE RIGHT MAN ON OUR SIDE,
THE MAN OF GOD'S OWN CHOOSING.
YOU ASK WHO THAT MAY BE?
CHRIST JESUS, IT IS HE;
LORD SABAOTH HIS NAME,
FROM AGE TO AGE THE SAME;
AND HE MUST WIN THE BATTLE.

AND THOUGH THIS WORLD, WITH DEVILS FILLED,
SHOULD THREATEN TO UNDO US,
WE WILL NOT FEAR, FOR GOD HAS WILLED
HIS TRUTH TO TRIUMPH THROUGH US.
THE PRINCE OF DARKNESS GRIM,
WE TREMBLE NOT FOR HIM;
HIS RAGE WE CAN ENDURE,
FOR LO! HIS DOOM IS SURE;
ONE LITTLE WORD SHALL FELL HIM.

THAT WORD ABOVE ALL EARTHLY POWERS—
NO THANKS TO THEM—ABIDETH;
THE SPIRIT AND THE GIFTS ARE OURS

THROUGH HIM WHO WITH US SIDETH.
LET GOODS AND KINDRED GO,
THIS MORTAL LIFE ALSO;
THE BODY THEY MAY KILL:
GOD'S TRUTH ABIDETH STILL;
HIS KINGDOM IS FOREVER!

—Martin Luther, 1529; tr. Frederick H. Hedge, 1852;
based on Psalm 46

I grew up singing this hymn, but I never really took the devil or his demons seriously until I began full-time Christian ministry in the city. After twenty-seven years of ministry in the city of Paterson, I know the devil and his hosts are real. The devil attacks cities because they influence the rest of our culture and world; as the city goes so the country goes.

The New York City metropolitan area where I live is one of the most influential areas in the world. It is a center of global finance, entertainment, arts, music, education, and international relations. What a great place for Satan to attack individuals and corporate structures of our society and world. The church of Jesus Christ must be aware of her enemy and ready to do battle.

What we believe about the reality of Satan and his hosts affects how we live as Christians. In this chapter, we will

▸ gain a biblical and confessional understanding of the reality of the devil and his hosts.
▸ develop an increased awareness of the devil's attacks and the defenses, including signs and wonders, with which Christ has equipped us to defeat Satan and his hosts.

BIBLICAL AND CONFESSIONAL UNDERSTANDING

Satan was an angel who rebelled against God. He was cast out of heaven and "hurled to the earth" (Rev. 12:7-9). Since the devil was once an angel, our study of the devil must begin with a review of angels. Angels are "ministering spirits sent to serve those who will inherit salvation" (Heb. 1:14). In the Bible, we see them giving

- direction (Gen. 16:9; Acts 8:26).
- comfort (1 Kings 19:4-8; Mark 1:12-13).
- protection (Ex. 14:19; Ps. 91:11).
- deliverance (Ps. 34:7; Dan. 6:22; Acts 5:19).
- judgment (Gen. 19; Matt. 13:41; 2 Thess. 1:7).
- messages from God himself (Gen. 18; Luke 2:9-14; Matt. 1:20).

THE DEVIL AND THE OLD TESTAMENT

Only a few direct references to Satan and his hosts are found in the Old Testament. John identifies the serpent in the Garden of Eden as "that ancient serpent called the devil, or Satan . . ." (Rev. 12:9) who tempted Adam and Eve to disobey God. God cursed the serpent and "put enmity" (Gen. 3:15) between Satan and all people.

In Job 1:7 we read that Satan was "roaming through the earth and going back and forth in it." He is also the cause of Job's loss of family, possessions, and health. In Zechariah 3:1-7 we see Satan accusing Joshua the high priest of his sin, but the Lord rebukes Satan and declares Joshua forgiven.

Communication with spirits and sorcerers was expressly forbidden by God, and the penalty for being a sorcerer was death (Ex. 22:18; Lev. 20:27). This is what the witch of Endor feared when Saul approached her to communicate with the spirit of Samuel (1 Sam. 28:7-24). Isaiah also warned against consulting mediums and spirits (8:19) and against looking for answers in sorcery, magic, and astrology (47:12-15) rather than in God.

THE DEVIL AND JESUS

In the New Testament, Jesus' ministry begins as Satan tempts him in the wilderness (Matt. 4:1-11). When confronted by an evil spirit during one of his first sermons, Jesus casts it out (Mark 1:21-28). Jesus continued to cast out demons throughout his ministry (Matt. 8:28-32; 12:22; 15:22-28; 17:14-18).

Jesus also gave his disciples authority to cast out demons (Matt. 10:8), which they continued to do as part of their ministry after his ascension (Acts 5:16; 16:16-18; 19:11). Jesus taught his disciples to pray, "Deliver us from the evil one" (Matt. 6:13), and warned of how Satan would seek to snatch away the Word that was sown (Matt. 13:19).

Jesus also accused Peter of being used by Satan (Mark 8:33) and said the Jews who opposed him belonged to "[their] father, the devil" (John

8:44). On one occasion, Jesus taught that Satan was the source of a woman's sickness (Luke 13:16).

Jesus taught that Satan was a "murderer from the beginning, not holding to the truth" (John 8:44), and the "prince of this world" who "now stands condemned" (John 14:30; 16:11). When accused of being Satan, Jesus declared that Beelzebub was the prince of demons and that his being driven out was a sign of the presence of the kingdom of God (Matt. 12:22-28).

THE DEVIL AND THE APOSTLES

The apostles recognized the ongoing work of Satan and his hosts in opposition to the gospel. John acknowledged that "the whole world is under the control of the evil one" (1 John 5:19) and warned that "he who does what is sinful is of the devil" (3:8).

Believers are called to "test the spirits to see whether they are from God" (1 John 4:1). This calls for Christians to be ready and alert to the devil's tricky schemes (1 Pet. 5:8; 2 Cor. 2:11) by resisting him and drawing near to God (James 4:7-8). Satan and his hosts will

▸ blind the minds of unbelievers (2 Cor. 4:4).
▸ disguise themselves as "servants of righteousness" (11:15).
▸ do "counterfeit miracles, signs and wonders, and . . . every sort of evil that deceives those who are perishing" (2 Thess. 2:9-10).

Satan also fans the flames of fallen human nature to increase sexual immorality (1 Cor. 7:5), anger (Eph. 4:26), pride (1 Tim. 3:6), bitter envy, and selfish ambition (James 3:14), to mention just a few.

As the early disciples recognized the power of Satan, they also recognized Jesus' victory over him. John affirmed that Jesus came to "destroy the devil's work" (1 John 3:8). He assures believers that they "have overcome the evil one" (1 John 2:13) and that "the one who is in you is greater than the one who is in the world" (1 John 4:4). Paul strengthens believers with the assurance that in Christ

▸ "we are more than conquerors . . . for neither angels nor demons . . . will be able to separate us from the love of God" (Rom. 8:37-39).
▸ we will see Satan crushed under our feet (Rom.16:20).
▸ we have been given all we need—the armor of God—to defeat the devil and his hosts (Eph. 6:10-18).

THE REALITY OF SPIRITUAL BEINGS: ANGELS AND DEMONS

In the above biblical review, we saw that spiritual beings exist and are both for and against God. John Calvin saw the ministry of angels as a source of encouragement to Christians and stated,

> So then, whatever is said concerning the ministry of angels, let us direct it to the end that, having banished all lack of trust, our hope in God may be more firmly established. Indeed these helps have been prepared for us by the Lord that we may not be frightened by the multitude of the enemy, as if they might prevail against his assistance, but that we may take refuge in that utterance of Elisha that "there are more for us than against" (II Kings 6:16).
>
> —*Institutes of the Christian Religion,*
> The Westminster Press, 1960, pp. 171-172.

In Calvin's day, as today, many believed that the realm of angels, demons, and evil spirits was metaphorical. Belief that they existed supposedly arose out of superstition or a lack of education. The Age of Reason and rising scholasticism in the church sought to do away with these ancient superstitions and relegated spiritual beings to good or bad impulses rather than actual beings. Calvin spoke harshly of such beliefs.

The seventeenth century Enlightenment continued to view the devil and his hosts as mythical negative symbols rather than real spiritual beings. The twentieth century demythologizing of Scripture also relegated all these beliefs to myth with no foundation in reality. Theologian Rudolph Bultman states

> Now that the forces and the laws of nature have been discovered, we can no longer believe in spirits, whether good or evil. It is impossible to use electric light and the wireless and to avail ourselves of modern medical and surgical discoveries and at the same time to believe in the New Testament world of spirits and miracles.
>
> —*Kerygma and Myth: A Theological Debate,*
> Harper and Row, 1961, pp. 4-5.

Unfortunately, many churches that pride themselves on being biblical have lost sight of the reality of Satan and his hosts. I've watched countless churches in the midst of deep conflicts and spiritual battles who never recognized the reality of Article 12 of the Belgic Confession that they professed to believe:

> The devils and evil spirits are so corrupt
> that they are enemies of God
> and of everything good.
> They lie in wait for the church
> and every member of it
> like thieves,
> with all their power,
> to destroy and spoil everything
> by their deceptions.

In seeking to identify the root of the devil's attack on their church and ministry, these troubled churches had endless business meetings, evaluations, consultations, and seminars, but they never had extended times of prayer and fasting.

If the denial of the devil is one extreme, a preoccupation with the devil is the other. We have seen that the New Testament emphasizes both the reality of Satan and his attacks *and* the Christian's victory over him. But some blame demons every time something goes wrong. Although Frank Peretti's bestselling Christian novels, such as *This Present Darkness*, alerted many to the reality of spiritual warfare, they verge on the extreme. The popular phrase "the devil made me do it" can become an excuse for people's own sin, blaming the devil for evil desires and actions that are really people's own responsibility. Rather than rebuking the demon of lust, for example, some may need to practice the spiritual gift of self-control by averting their eyes and walking in another direction.

C. S. Lewis warns against either of these extremes:

> There are two equal and opposite errors into which our race can fall about the devils. One is to disbelieve in their existence. The other is to believe and to feel an excessive and unhealthy interest in them. They themselves are equally pleased by both errors and hail a materialist or a magician with the same delight.
>
> —*The Screwtape Letters*, Barbour and Co., 1990, p. 9.

At War with the Devil

As we saw in chapter 5, Jesus ushered in the kingdom of God, though it will not be completed until he returns. This victory is seen in Jesus' authority over Satan, demons, and evil spirits. The binding of Satan mentioned in Revelation 20 is completed. Although he still has power, Satan is ultimately under God's control. Oscar Cullman describes this binding of Satan and his hosts in this way:

> In the time between the resurrection and the parousia of Christ they are, so to speak, bound as to a rope, which can be more or less lengthened, so that those among them who show tendencies to emancipation can have the illusion that they are releasing themselves from their bond with Christ, which in reality, by this striving which here and there appears, they only show once more their original demonic character; they cannot, however, actually set themselves free. Their power is only an apparent power.
>
> —*Christ and Time*, The Westminster Press, 1960, p. 198.

In giving his disciples authority over demons and evil spirits, Jesus equipped them to be involved in this spiritual battle. In the same way that we apply the great commission to our lives today as a call to evangelize and disciple the nations, we must also recognize Jesus' commission to heal the sick and cast out demons. When Jesus sent out the twelve and the seventy-two disciples on their mission, he gave them authority to heal and to exorcize evil spirits.

In his book *Christianity with Power* (Servant Publications, 1989, p. 71), Charles Kraft offers some practical suggestions on what this means for Christians today:

> So how should we act in the war? First, we are to recognize the fact that there is a war going on. . . . Second, we are to recognize that the war is taking place in the enemy's territory. Jesus calls Satan "the ruler of this world" (John 14:30). . . . Third, we need to recognize that we—the followers of Christ—are automatically enlisted in his army. . . . Fourth, we know for sure who is going to win the war. . . . Therefore, we can fight with gladness and confidence, rather than with fear.

I tell my congregation, "Where sin abounds, demons hang out." In recognizing the reality of demonic spirits, the best way to stay free of them is through holy Christian living. As we live and walk in our position with Christ, who is seated at God's right hand, we walk in the authority of Christ over all the attacks of the enemy.

THE WORLD, THE FLESH, AND THE DEVIL

In Ephesians 2:1-2, the apostle Paul writes about the relationship of the world, the flesh, and the devil in the lives of unbelievers: "As for you, you were dead in your transgressions and sins, in which you used to live when you followed the ways of this world and of the ruler of the kingdom of the air, the spirit who is now at work in those who are disobedient."

John also refers to this threefold relationship throughout his first epistle: "For everything in the world—the cravings of sinful man, the lust of his eyes and the boasting of what he has and does—comes not from the Father but from the world" (1 John 2:16). John says Cain murdered Abel because he "belonged to the evil one" (3:12). In Genesis, God warned Cain that "sin is crouching at your door; it desires to have you, but you must master it" (Gen. 4:6-7).

Jesus' temptation by Satan also demonstrates the relationship between the flesh (hunger), the world (power), and the devil. Jesus' temptation in the wilderness teaches us to

- be ready for Satan's attacks.
- be alert to Satan's schemes.
- be aware of our own human weakness.
- know and use Scripture.
- listen to the voice of God.

The Heidelberg Catechism recognizes this relationship in Question and Answer 127 (see "Reformed Reflections" at the end of this chapter) when it says, ". . . our sworn enemies—the devil, the world, and our own flesh—never stop attacking us." This recognition of the Christian's battle with the devil is also described in Question and Answer 32 (see "Reformed Reflections" in chapter 8).

The Reformed tradition has emphasized our battle with and victory over "the world and our own flesh" but has too often overlooked our battle with the devil. This strategic omission may relate more to worldview than to theological beliefs, but to live in victory we must recognize the reality of our battle against Satan. Not only is this biblical, but it is also part of our Reformed tradition and confessions. As John Calvin said, "The fact that the devil is everywhere called God's adversary and ours also ought to fire us to an unceasing struggle against him" (*Institutes of the Christian Religion*, The Westminster Press, 1960, p. 174).

DEMONS AND DELIVERANCE

One area of spiritual warfare that needs special attention is deliverance from demons or evil spirits. Some psychologists, such as M. Scott Peck, are beginning to recognize thie spiritual reality. Peck "met Satan" in an exorcism and became convinced that "there is some relationship between Satanic activity and human evil" (*People of the Lie*, Simon and Schuster, 1983, p. 184).

When Craig Ellison and Edward S. Maynard published their book *Healing for the City* (Zondervan, 1992), they included a chapter on demon possession and deliverance. Dr. Ellison personally shared with me how much criticism they received from the psychological community for believing that demons existed. In a recent conversation with a Christian counselor, I suggested that a besetting sin problem might be the result of demonic attack. Although he was open to the suggestion, he did not think many of his colleagues at his Christian mental health center would share such a perspective.

Throughout history, people have turned to the Christian church for help with demons and evil spirits. In fact, the baptism liturgies of the early church recognized the reality of Satan and his hosts and included exorcism as preparation for baptism. Exorcism is widely practiced in Pentecostal and charismatic churches and is still part of the liturgy in the Roman Catholic and Orthodox churches. Following is an excerpt from the form for exorcism prior to baptism in Orthodox churches:

> Be rebuked and go out, unclean spirit. For I adjure you by him who walked on the surface of the sea as if upon dry land, and rebuked the storm of winds, whose glance dries up abysses, and whose threat dissolves mountains. For heaven now commands you through us. Be afraid, go out, and leave these creatures and do not return or hide in them or encounter any of them or work upon them or attack them either by night or by day or at the hour of noon. Be afraid of God, who sits upon a throne . . . before whom the heaven trembles and the earth and the

sea and all that are in them. Go out and depart from the sealed, newly chosen soldiers of Christ our God . . . because the name of the Father and of the Son and of the Holy Spirit has been glorified now and forever and for all ages of ages. Amen.

—Henry Ansgar Kelly, *The Devil at Baptism: Ritual, Theology, and Drama,* Cornell University Press, 1985, p. 164.

The Christian Reformed Church's report on Neo-Pentecostalism urged caution in this area but concluded with these words of positive encouragement:

We believe that as the last days draw to their close, there may be a noticeable increase in demon possession. We caution against the too hasty assumption that most cases of moral lapse and resistance to the gospel are instances of demon possession, but we call upon the church to exorcise such cases of true demon possession as may come to its attention with unerring fidelity to Christ and the Scriptures.

—*Acts of Synod 1973,* Christian Reformed Church in North America, 1973, p. 463.

The question of whether Christians can be possessed by demons has sparked much debate among Christians who are involved in deliverance ministries. The Bible teaches that "the one who is in you is greater than the one who is in the world" (1 John 4:4). This seems to imply that the Holy Spirit and an evil spirit cannot occupy the same body. In the New Testament, we know of no cases where demons were cast out of Christians. But throughout church history and today there are testimonies of Christians who struggle with demons or evil spirits.

To explain this, distinctions have been made between demon *possession* and demon *oppression*, recognizing that while demons may oppress, they cannot possess a Christian. More recently, several theologians have recognized that the Greek word *daimonizomai* is better translated *demonization*. This recognizes a spectrum of demonic intensity from mild attacks to complete possession. Christians may not be completely possessed, but they can certainly be attacked.

This area requires much caution and spiritual discernment. Discernment is one of the gifts of the Holy Spirit and should be applied to demonization. In the same way that we must not negate the reality of the *demoni,* neither should we label every temptation, sinful human desire, or corrupt influence of the world as a demon. Demons often revealed themselves to

Jesus; he did not have to go hunting for them. Christian counselors Craig Ellison and Edward Maynard offer the following advice:

> There seem to be certain characteristics that suggest the presence of the demonic. Two important differences exist between multiple personality disorder and the demonic. First, in MPD the personalities are not aware of each other. In demonization not only may the two be aware of each other, but they may communicate with each other. Second, in demonization, the "other person" is evil. Another characteristic of demonization is the individual's reaction to the name of Jesus . . . demons today react negatively and sometimes even violently to his name. A final characteristic of the demonic involves the biblical injunction to "test the spirits" (1 John 4:1). . . . After careful assessment, if it appears likely that the problem is demonic, more direct evaluation and possible deliverance can begin.
> —*Healing for the City,* Zondervan Publishing House, 1992, pp. 99-100.

TERRITORIAL SPIRITS

A final word should be said about territorial spirits that seem to inhabit certain places and objects. We find only implied biblical teaching about this (in Daniel 10:13—the NIV footnotes say "the prince of the Persian kingdom" apparently refers to a demon), but there are many examples of actual experience. We must be aware of these territorial spirits if the gospel is to be effectively proclaimed.

In the mission field, Christians often notice that certain places and objects seem to be particularly occupied by evil spirits and demons. Some suggest that the lack of conversions in Japan, after centuries of intense missionary effort, is due to territorial spirits.

One Food for the Hungry missionary shared with me his experience in a demon-worshiping village in Kenya. The demon was apparently very angry about the missionary's efforts to bring the gospel, and tried in many ways to drive him out. Finally, after the missionary and other Christian believers drove the demon out of the village, many came to Christ.

Recently a prayer team of clergy from our city prayed on top of Garrett Mountain which overlooks the city of Paterson. We prayed to discern what territorial spirits were holding the city in spiritual and economic bondage. As we prayed, we sensed the Holy Spirit pointing us to

Paterson's history. Paterson was one of the first planned industrial cities in the United States, and its labor has been at the hands of poor immigrants who were exploited to the benefit of the wealthy. We believe these sins of the past were exacerbated by demonic attack and possession and that they need to be identified, confessed, and finally cast out. This requires prayerful discernment and persistence.

In exploring the biblical references to judgments and blessings on the land, Randy Woodley brings a unique perspective:

> We can surely expect Satan to move in on any territory with an atmosphere that welcomes him. We sometimes think of demons as forcing their way in on us, but the idea of demonic intruders is somewhat of a misnomer. An intruder is someone unwelcome. When we abandon our posts as God's good stewards of any area of the Kingdom of God, including territory that formerly welcomed God, we block his needed hand of protection and invite an onslaught of demonic infestation.
> —*Living in Color,* InterVarsity Press, 2001, p. 160.

In this chapter we have seen the biblical reality of the devil and evil spirits. As Christians, we must be aware of their attacks and of the spiritual resources that Jesus gives us to defend against them and to defeat them. Jesus said to Peter, "I will build my church, and the gates of Hades will not overcome it" (Matt. 16:18) Jesus was teaching his disciples that the church would offensively attack the gates of hell and not be defeated.

We live in the spiritual reality of Jesus' defeat of Satan, but we remain under attack until Christ comes again. This is lived out in daily battles against the devil and his hosts and by walking in the spiritual authority that is ours in Christ Jesus.

TESTIMONIES FROM . . .

DR. WILBUR PICKERING (1963)

When Dr. Wilbur Pickering and his wife reached the upper Amazon in 1963 to begin their missionary career, they knew exactly what they would do. He would begin translating Scripture portions into the language of the Apurina Indians. He knew these primitive people were animists. Demons were central to all their activities. Birth, death, marriage, child rearing, fishing, and food gathering were all in some way related to their spirit world. As Dr. Pickering related the task to his thorough training in theology, linguistics and anthropology, he was confident he could do the job. One day as Dr. Pickering was walking through the village, he suddenly fell to the ground with acute abdominal pain. The pain subsided and he got up, only to be thrown to the ground with the same pain. By now, Indian bystanders were laughing at him. Dr. Pickering got up and went on his way, completely baffled by his strange experience. Later, to his astonishment and shame, Dr. Pickering realized he had been attacked by demons. The laughing Indians knew very well what was going on, even though he did not. Forced to rethink the reality of the spirit world, he opened his Bible and began a serious study of supernatural power. Later, he lamented that he had not been as effective in evangelizing the Apurinas as he might have been, had he been trained to work with the spiritual powers he encountered there.

—Neuza Itioka, "Mission in the 1990s: Two Views, " *International Bulletin of Missionary Research*, Vol. 14, No. 1, Jan. 7-10, 1990, pp. 7-8.

DAVE AND JAN DYKGRAFF (1992)

A small young girl had been in labor for 24 hours with her first child when missionary Jan Dykgraaf was called to the compound [in Idaci, Nigeria]. . . . Everyone knew something was wrong. The baby was not coming. They took the girl and walked her around the compound, but the baby still did not come, and the girl was very weak. Even after a woman baptized the girl and prayed to God, there was no baby. Two senior wives suddenly jumped up and started marching around the compound, throwing their arms out and shouting in the darkness for the ancestors to leave. Then women inside a spirit cult started calling to that spirit. When two more women came across the field hysterically laughing like hyenas and one with two machetes leaped after the girl, Jan and Dave took action. "Following Jesus' example, Dave, filled with power and authority, bound all the evil spirits around us and sent them away," Jan says. "They went! Immediately it was calm, and we directed our prayers to God in Jesus' name for the girl and the yet unborn baby. Before we stopped praying, a healthy baby boy was born!" Everyone in the compound was shocked, and Dave and Jan were humbled that God worked through them in such a marvelous way. When they were thanked for the baby, they gave the praise to God alone and spent the next hour talking with the people, telling them that God's power is above any evil and they must pray to God alone in Jesus' name. The next morning, they talked again with the compound head about clearing the compound of evil. The next Sunday, two women from Idaci went with the Dykgraffs for the first time to worship at the church in Maido.

—*Christian Reformed World Missions: Prayer Needs and Praises*,
Christian Reformed World Missions, 1992, p. 2.

REFORMED REFLECTIONS

THE BELGIC CONFESSION, ARTICLE 12

He has also created the angels good,
that they might be his messengers
and serve his elect.
Some of them have fallen
from the excellence in which God created them
into eternal perdition;

And the others have persisted and remained
   in their original state,
   by the grace of God.

The devils and evil spirits are so corrupt
that they are enemies of God
and of everything good.
They lie in wait for the church
and every member of it
like thieves,
   with all their power,
to destroy and spoil everything
      by their deceptions.

So then,
by their own wickedness
they are condemned to everlasting damnation,
   daily awaiting their torments.

Reflect on some ways that "the devils and evil spirits . . . lie in wait
   for [your] church" or "spoil everything by their deceptions."

THE HEIDELBERG CATECHISM, Q&A 127
Q. What does the sixth request mean?

A. *And lead us not into temptation,*
   but deliver us from the evil one means,

By ourselves we are too weak
to hold our own even for a moment.

And our sworn enemies—
the devil, the world, and our own flesh—
never stop attacking us.

And so, Lord,
uphold us and make us strong
with the strength of your Holy Spirit,
so that we may not go down to defeat
in this spiritual struggle,
but may firmly resist our enemies
until we finally win the complete victory.

> Reflect on how you are resisting the devil,
> the world, and your own flesh.

QUESTIONS TO THINK ABOUT

▸ Do you believe that the devil, evil spirits, and demons are real spiritual beings? Why or why not?

▸ Have you ever seen concrete evidence of demons? Explain.

▸ How did Jesus' temptations correspond to the world, the flesh, and the devil?

▸ What are some of the devil's "schemes" as referred to in Ephesians 6:11?

▸ What are some current examples of "the flaming arrows of the evil one" as referred to in Ephesians 6:16?

PRAYER AND PRACTICE

Pray aloud Paul's prayer to the Philippians:

And this is my prayer: that your love may abound more and more in knowledge and depth of insight, so that you may be able to discern what is best and may be pure and blameless until the day of Christ, filled with the fruit of righteousness that comes through Jesus Christ—to the glory and praise of God.
—Philippians 1:9-11

Identify three areas in your life where you recognize Satan's attacks; pray about them, asking the Spirit to help you defeat the devil.

ADDITIONAL RESOURCES

BOOKS

▸ Anderson, Neil. *The Bondage Breaker.* Eugene, Ore.: Harvest House, 1990.
▸ ———. *Victory Over the Darkness.* Ventura, Calif.: Regal Books, 1990.
▸ Stam, Jeff. *Straight Talk About Spiritual Warfare.* Grand Rapids. Mich.: Faith Alive Christian Resources, 1999.
▸ Warner, Timothy. *Spiritual Warfare.* Wheaton, Ill.: Crossway Books, 1991.
▸ White, Thomas B. *The Believer's Guide to Spiritual Warfare.* Ann Arbor, Mich.: Servant Publications, 1990.

TRAINING RESOURCE

"Equipping for Spiritual Warfare," The Dunamis Project: Dunamis V Training Seminar. www.prmi.org.

CHAPTER TEN

DISCERNING THE SPIRITS: DANGERS AND CAUTIONS

THE CHURCH'S ONE FOUNDATION IS JESUS CHRIST, HER LORD;
SHE IS HIS NEW CREATION BY WATER AND THE WORD.
FROM HEAVEN HE CAME AND SOUGHT HER TO BE HIS HOLY BRIDE;
WITH HIS OWN BLOOD HE BOUGHT HER, AND FOR HER LIFE HE DIED.

ELECT FROM EVERY NATION, YET ONE O'ER ALL THE EARTH;
HER CHARTER OF SALVATION: ONE LORD, ONE FAITH, ONE BIRTH.
ONE HOLY NAME SHE BLESSES, PARTAKES ONE HOLY FOOD,
AND TO ONE HOPE SHE PRESSES, WITH EVERY GRACE ENDUED.

THOUGH WITH A SCORNFUL WONDER THE WORLD SEES
HER OPPRESSED,
BY SCHISMS RENT ASUNDER, BY HERESIES DISTRESSED,
YET SAINTS THEIR WATCH ARE KEEPING; THEIR CRY GOES UP:
"HOW LONG?"
AND SOON THE NIGHT OF WEEPING SHALL BE THE MORN OF SONG.

MID TOIL AND TRIBULATION, AND TUMULT OF HER WAR,
SHE WAITS THE CONSUMMATION OF PEACE FOREVERMORE,
TILL WITH THE VISION GLORIOUS HER LONGING EYES ARE BLEST,
AND THE GREAT CHURCH VICTORIOUS SHALL BE THE CHURCH
AT REST.

—Samuel J. Stone, 1866

For my twenty-fifth anniversary in ministry our congregation gave my wife and me a trip to Colorado. We drove the "million-dollar highway" from Silverton to Durango, an area called "little Switzerland." Along this highway is some of the most spectacular scenery in North America, but it is full of warnings: "Steep Drop," "Dangerous Curves," "Watch for Falling Rocks."

Exploring the mighty acts of God and their ongoing place in our lives is similar. This is the road God takes, so we don't want to miss it. On the other hand, we're sure to encounter falling rocks and dangerous curves. How many internationally known "faith healers" have mismanaged finances? How many televangelists are getting rich by promising health and wealth in exchange for a "seed" offering? How many revivals include strange manifestations of laughter, slaying in the spirit, and other excesses that leave us puzzled? How many bad theologies blame people for their lack of faith and make the sick feel guilty? How many people use demons as an excuse for their own disobedient behavior?

These are just a few of my own questions. I know you have yours as well. In this section, we will identify some areas of concern to be considered when putting into practice the principles we have discussed. These include

- false teaching
- bad theology
- counterfeit miracles
- seeking the spectacular
- pride and power
- empty emotionalism

It is my prayer that you will recognize the common theological errors and practical dangers related to signs and wonders as you use the spiritual gift of discernment.

FALSE TEACHING

The Bible is clear that false teachers and prophets will seek to lead God's people astray. In the Old Testament, we're told about those claiming to be prophets of God who were not and others who were prophets but spoke falsely. To refute the lies of 400 other prophets, Micaiah spoke the true Word of God to Saul, even though it was not what Saul wanted to hear (1 Kings 22). During the siege of Jerusalem, Jeremiah lamented: "A horrible and shocking thing has happened in the land: The prophets prophesy lies, the priests rule by their own authority" (Jer. 5: 30-31).

In the New Testament, Jesus warns: "Many will say to me on that day, 'Lord, Lord, did we not prophesy in your name, and in your name drive out demons and perform many miracles?' Then I will tell them plainly, 'I never knew you. Away from me, you evildoers!'" (Matt. 7:22-23). Jesus also teaches that the end of the age will be marked by false prophets and teachers identifying themselves as Christ himself to deceive many. "For false Christs and false prophets will appear and perform great signs and miracles to deceive even the elect—if that were possible" (Matt. 24:24).

The disciple John warned believers "not to believe every spirit but test the spirits to see whether they are from God, because many false prophets have gone out into the world" (1 John 4:1). Like Jeremiah and Micaiah, John recognizes that Satan sends out lying evil spirits to distort the truth through false teaching and prophecy. John tells us to test the spirits to discern if they confess that Jesus "has come in the flesh from God" (v. 2) and if they recognize the truth of God's Word (v. 6).

Paul also warned the Corinthians against false teaching (2 Cor. 11:3-4) and those masquerading as "servants of righteousness" (vv. 13-15). Paul charges Timothy as a minister of the Word to guard against false teachers who may be led by "deceiving spirits and things taught by demons" (1 Tim. 4:1). This warning recognizes the danger of those who look for "teachers to say what their itching ears want to hear" (2 Tim. 4:3) rather than the truth.

The growth of the New Testament church was accompanied by false teaching and heresy that still has modern counterparts. The Nicene and Athanasian Creeds of the fourth century sought to clarify the truths of orthodox Christianity in reaction to Arianism (denying the three persons of the Trinity) and Modalism (denying one God). The Reformation of the sixteenth century was in reaction to false teaching and practice of the Roman Catholic Church and brought about renewed biblical teaching and practice. But it, too, was followed by an abundance of false teaching within Protestantism as well as Catholicism. The writings of the Heidelberg Catechism, the Belgic Confession, the Westminster Confession, and the Canons of Dort were an effort to define "true Christianity." The Canons evidence this reaction to false teaching in the "Rejection of Errors" that accompanies each head of doctrine.

Times of revival during the Great Awakenings were often accompanied by false teaching and religious fanaticism. Church historian Richard Lovelace identifies the dangers of false teaching and mistaken theology as strategies of Satan to

▸ destroy the work either by persecution or by accusation which will discredit it and limit its growth.
▸ infiltrate the work and reinforce its defects in order to provide more evidence for accusation.
▸ inspire counterfeit revival which may deceive the elect and further confuse and alienate the on-looking world.
—*Dynamics of Spiritual Life*, InterVarsity Press, 1979, p. 257.

When signs and wonders are emphasized by Christian churches today, many of these defects continue to appear; they range from mildly mistaken theology to total heresy. Rather than discerning what is false and celebrating what is real, the response is often to "throw the baby out with the bath water."

BAD THEOLOGY

Much false teaching and bad theology arise out of biblical exegesis gone wrong. Related to the manifestation of signs and wonders, the "Word of Faith" movement has credited our faith for getting God to do whatever it is we want God to do. Claiming biblical precedent in Mark 11:24 where Jesus says, "Therefore I tell you, whatever you ask for in prayer, believe that you have received it, and it will be yours," this movement teaches that faith expressed in positive statements of what we believe in accord with God's Word makes our desires realities.

One dimension of this teaching is that God wants everyone to be healthy and wealthy. Therefore, a person's quality of life is dependent on his or her level of faith; if a person is not healed or does not prosper financially, something must be lacking in that person's faith. Such bad theology can lead to a denial of reality. Lawrence Parker and his wife made national news when as an act of faith they threw away their son's insulin because a visiting evangelist claimed he was healed from diabetes. Their son died a few days later. In an article titled "Bad Theology Can Kill," Lewis Smedes concludes: "Lawrence Parker did not draw a bizarre conclusion from a good theology; he drew a consistent conclusion from a bad theology. He went the full route of a misled faith. His son died of bad theology" *(The Reformed Journal,* 1973, 23:8, pp. 7-8.)

Making healing or blessings contingent on faith also leads to self-destructive guilt or God-denying cynicism. Everything is reduced to a simple "faith formula," which if followed will always bring the desired result. Guilt is added to sickness as the person must bear the blame and responsibility for not having enough faith. Others are left feeling angry with God for not answering their demands that were made in faith. Some Christians have been scarred deeply because they followed the right "faith formula" but did not get what they wanted.

Another text often quoted in this movement is Jesus' words in Matthew 18:19: "I tell you that if two of you on earth agree about anything you ask for, it will be done for you by my Father in heaven." Again, this verse is ripped from its context related to restoring a sinful brother and applied as a "faith formula" for getting us anything we want. This is a clear example of culture exegeting the Scriptures rather than Scripture speaking to culture.

COUNTERFEIT MIRACLES

Not all signs, wonders, and miracles are from God or to the glory of God. In the Old Testament, the magicians of Egypt duplicated Moses' miracles of turning water to blood and staffs to serpents (Ex. 7). In the New Testament, Jesus says that some false prophets will be able to do miraculous signs and wonders, acting as though they are part of the kingdom (Matt. 24:23-24). Jesus teaches us to discern those who are truly God's servants as those who do "the will of my Father who is in heaven" (Matt. 7:21).

Paul warned the Thessalonians that "the coming of the lawless one will be in accordance with the work of Satan displayed in all kinds of counterfeit miracles, signs and wonders, and in every sort of evil that deceives those who are perishing" (2 Thess. 2:9-10). The devil himself will use false miracles to confuse the saints and attack the gospel.

This is one reason why church fathers of the first few centuries sought to confirm and record miracles. Then, as now, it was important to distinguish the miracles of God from the miracles of the devil. We must recognize that not everything that can be called a sign and wonder may be a miracle of God or give glory to God.

In the Reformed community, the teaching of theologian Benjamin B. Warfield and his book *Counterfeit Miracles* (The Banner of Truth Trust,

1972) had tremendous influence in convincing many that God no longer did miracles. This cessationist view is an extreme reaction to the danger of abuse and the reality of counterfeit miracles by saying that God no longer works in such a way.

SEEKING THE SPECTACULAR

Another "caution sign" on the road of God's signs and wonders is the human tendency to seek the spectacular. Jesus willingly did signs and wonders on many occasions, yet refused to do them to satisfy the appetites of those who were only looking for a spectacular show. "This is a wicked generation. It asks for a miraculous sign, but none will be given it except the sign of Jonah," Jesus said (Luke 11:29). Jesus refused to do a miracle for Herod (23:8-9) or to respond to the crowd's taunting him to come down from the cross (Matt. 27:39-40). Jesus clearly states that the purpose of miracles is to give glory to the Father (John 15:8). Jesus also commended those who believed without seeing (20:29).

In contrast to the Jews' thirst for miraculous signs and the Greeks' search for wisdom, Paul stressed "Christ the power of God and the wisdom of God" (1 Cor. 1:22-24). The thirst for miraculous signs is a very real danger today as well. In our entertainment-centered culture, everybody likes to see something they've never seen before. Our society craves experiences that are dramatic, shocking, novel, and larger-than-life.

This attitude leads people to easily lose sight of God's ongoing work in the world. Recently an internationally known healing ministry invited people in the Paterson area to come and "Claim your miracle!" Sometimes I have watched religious leaders revving people up to an ecstatic frenzy as they call on God to do signs and wonders. They put more emphasis on the "manifestations" than on the holiness of God. The services remind me of Elijah's word to the prophets of Baal when no fire came from heaven: "Shout louder!" (1 Kings 18:27). But when it was Elijah's turn—after the altars were drenched with water—he prayed this simple prayer:

> "O LORD, God of Abraham, Isaac and Israel, let it be known today that you are God in Israel and that I am your servant and have done all these things at your command. Answer me, O LORD, answer me, so these people will know that you, O LORD, are God, and that you are turning their hearts back again."
> —1 Kings 18:36-37

In recounting the many manifestations and works of God in his own parish of Northampton, Massachusetts, during the Great Awakening of 1740-1742, Jonathan Edwards lamented years later that the change that seemed to occur in so many people's lives was short-lived. This did not mean that the change was not real, but it reminds us again that signs, wonders, and manifestations of the Spirit of God—if unaccompanied by ongoing Christian discipleship—will have little lasting impact.

We must be careful to seek *God*, not seek just signs and wonders. We must also be careful about making distinctions between the *supernatural* and *natural* work of God. Although God demonstrated his power in a spectacular way for Elijah over the prophets of Baal, God also daily equipped Elijah to speak ordinary words to ordinary people (and often without extraordinary results).

PRIDE AND POWER

To be able to pray and see the sick healed, to speak and see demons cast out, to preach and see people born again of the Spirit of God is a tremendous privilege. But when we allow our own pride and power to enter the picture, God is not honored. Neither the Old Testament prophets of God nor the New Testament disciples of Jesus were at liberty to perform signs and wonders or to use spiritual gifts for their own gain or benefit. Neither are we today.

Shortly after Jesus cast out a demon that his disciples were unable to cast out (Mark 9:14-32), they began to argue about who was the greatest. One can imagine, knowing human pride, the accusations that followed their inability to do this exorcism:

▶ "You should have let *me* do it."
▶ "You didn't pray enough!"
▶ "You prayed too much!"
▶ "You needed to declare it was done."

Jesus, knowing human nature and his disciples' tendency toward pride and power, proceeded to teach them about being servants and being like children (Mark 9:35-37). He teaches us this as well.

The apostle Paul spends three chapters in 1 Corinthians instructing about spiritual gifts and addressing the danger of spiritual "elitism" into which many Christians had fallen. Though recognizing the importance of the gifts of tongues, prophecy, faith, and giving, Paul stresses that without love one is nothing more than a "resounding gong or a clanging cymbal" (1 Cor.13:1). To those who take pride in speaking in tongues, Paul declares the importance of prophecy and interpretation because they edify the church (14:5). The gifts of the Spirit are given so that "the body of Christ may be built up" (Eph. 4:12), "for the common good" (1 Cor. 12:7), and "to serve others" (1 Pet. 4:10). Signs and wonders that serve these purposes are done in the context of God's will and for God's glory. Spiritual pride contradicts this important biblical truth and loses sight of the greatest gift of love.

The twin of pride is power. This seems to be the sin of Moses when, instead of speaking to the rock as God instructed him, he said, "Listen, you rebels, must we bring you water out of this rock?" (Num. 20:10); then he struck the rock with his staff. Moses was the man with the rod of God called to show the people God's power, not his own.

Jesus' disciples were no different. On one occasion when a Samaritan village did not welcome Jesus, James and John asked, "Lord, do you want us to call fire down from heaven to destroy them?" (Luke 9:54). These brothers, called "Sons of Thunder," seemed to have some power issues. Jesus rebuked them and went on his way.

Jesus had the power to give King Herod a spectacular demonstration and to remove himself from the cross, yet he did not. Recognizing that God's power is ours through the Holy Spirit, we must avoid misusing that power for our own selfish gain.

In the book of Acts, Simon the Sorcerer was known as "the Great Power" in Samaria. After believing the gospel and being baptized, Simon became impressed with the greater power of the disciples, especially as he watched people receive the Holy Spirit. When Simon inquired about purchasing this ability, Peter responded harshly:

> "May your money perish with you, because you thought you could buy the gift of God with money! You have no part or share in this ministry, because your heart is not right before God. Repent of this wickedness and pray to the Lord. Perhaps he will forgive you for having such a thought in your heart. For I see that you are full of bitterness and captive to sin."
> —Acts 8:20-23

The motive of our hearts is so important. Involvement in a power ministry leaves one especially vulnerable to these temptations of pride and power. From the days of the early church to the present, Christian leaders have often succumbed to the temptations of pride, money, and abuse of spiritual power.

EMPTY EMOTIONALISM

Emotions, a gift from God, are inseparable from our experience of God's grace and gifts in our lives. But emotions alone, without real content, are dangerous.

Paul's warnings about speaking in tongues and disorderly worship hint of wild emotions without solid foundations (1 Cor. 14). On the other hand, the believers in Berea "examined the Scriptures every day to see if what Paul said was true" (Acts 17:11). Theology must arise from the Word of God and not merely from the experiences of faith. This has been a problem throughout church history.

During the Great Awakening of 1740 in the Northampton, Massachusetts, parish of Jonathan Edwards, many accused him of excessive emotionalism and lack of control. In response, he wrote a treatise called "The Distinguishing Marks of a Work of the Spirit of God." One of Edwards' arguments stated: "It is not a sign that a work is not from the Spirit of God that many who seem to be the subjects of it are guilty of great imprudences and irregularities in their conduct " (*Jonathan Edwards on Revival,* Banner of Truth Trust, 1965, p. 104).

Today such dangers also exist. Emotional experiences can become delusions that are promoted as a new revelation. All must be tested and discerned in alignment with the Word of God as well as with the Spirit's illumination. Faith includes our feelings and our minds. When emotional experiences become substitute "highs" for the practice of daily Christian living, there is a problem.

Many of the African American members of our congregation joined because they were frustrated by what they considered the empty emotionalism of other churches they had attended. They watched people "get happy in the Spirit," then run around the church as if in an ecstatic trance, only to leave and act as un-Christlike as they had before. This emotionalism was a substitute for the content and life-changing power of the Word of God. Clearly we need both.

I'll never forget my life history interview with Rev. Miquel Mena, the pastor of the first and largest Latino Pentecostal church in the city of Paterson. As a Reformed pastor seeking to learn from my Pentecostal brother, I asked him how you really discern if something is from the Spirit of God, from one's own spirit, or from an evil spirit or false prophet. Pastor Mena kept repeating 1 John 4:1-2: "Test the spirits to see whether they are from God. . . . Every spirit that acknowledges that Jesus Christ has come in the flesh is from God." I wish now that I had pushed him harder on exactly how to test the spirits of those who acknowledge this but exhibit some of the other concerns we have just examined. Clearly, this testing is easier said than done, and should lead us to eagerly desire the spiritual gift of discernment in today's world.

It is amazing that God allows us to participate in signs and wonders through the gifts and movement of the Holy Spirit. This is a great privilege that we must handle with care. For this reason we are warned against the dangers of false teaching and bad theology. We are also warned against the dangers of counterfeit miracles, seeking the spectacular, pride and power, and empty emotionalism. Let us heed the danger signs as we travel this glorious road of discipleship.

TESTIMONIES FROM . . .

DR. PAUL BRAND (1983)

David Gilmore told about an illness of his fifteen-month-old son, Dustin Graham Gilmore, that began in April 1978. At first the child came down with flu-like symptoms. The Gilmores took him to their church, and the pastor prayed for him. Members of that church believed that faith alone heals any disease and that to look elsewhere for help—for example, to medical doctors—demonstrates a lack of faith in God. Gilmore and his wife followed the church's advice and simply prayed for their son. Over the next weeks they prayed faithfully as his temperature climbed, prayed when they noticed he no longer responded to sounds, and prayed harder when he went blind. On the morning of May 15, 1978, the day after the pastor preached an especially rousing sermon about faith, the Gilmores went into their son's room and found his body a blue color, and still. He was dead. Again they prayed, for their church also believed the power of prayer can raise the dead. But Dustin Graham Gilmore stayed dead. An autopsy revealed the infant died from a form of meningitis that could have been treated easily.

—"A Surgeon's View of Divine Healing,"
Christianity Today, Nov. 25, 1983, p. 14.

DR. LEWIS SMEDES (1987)

Students of our culture tell us that most modern Americans believe they have an inalienable right to personal fulfillment and happiness. Entitlement to a pain-free, disappointment-free, and frustration-free life, they tell us, has become a basic tenet of our time. Not duty but rights, not commitment but self-maximization, not the possibility of patient suffering but the guarantee of instant entitlement—these are the creeds of what Robert Bellah calls our "therapeutic culture." We cannot avoid the question whether the current Christian expectation of miraculous healing manifests the same syndrome. Do some aspects of the current healing movement encourage and perhaps express the cultural creed of personal entitlements?

—*Ministry and the Miraculous*, Fuller Theological Seminary, 1987, p. 78.

REFORMED REFLECTION

OUR WORLD BELONGS TO GOD: A CONTEMPORARY TESTIMONY, STANZA 43

We grieve that the church
which shares one Spirit, one faith, one hope,
and spans all time, place, race, and language
has become a broken communion in a broken world.
When we struggle for the purity of the church
and for the righteousness God demands,
we pray for saintly courage.
When our pride or blindness blocks
the unity of God's household,
we seek forgiveness.
We marvel that the Lord gathers the broken pieces
to do his work,
and that he blesses us still
with joy, new members,
and surprising evidences of unity.
We commit ourselves to seeking and expressing
the oneness of all who follow Jesus.

Reflect on how your "pride or blindness blocks the unity of God's household" and on how you can commit yourself to "seeking and expressing the oneness of all who follow Jesus."

QUESTIONS TO THINK ABOUT

▸ We've discussed the dangers we may encounter when signs and wonders are performed. What examples of these dangers have you witnessed or experienced in terms of
  • false teaching?
  • bad theology?
  • counterfeit miracles?
  • seeking the spectacular?
  • pride and power?
  • empty emotionalism?
▸ How have these experiences affected your desire for spiritual gifts? (See 1 Cor. 14:1).
▸ How do you "discern the spirits" (1 John 4:1-3)?

PRAYER AND PRACTICE

Pray aloud this psalm, a call to the nations to praise the Lord as the only God and to proclaim the glory of God's reign throughout the world:

> Sing to the LORD a new song;
> sing to the LORD, all the earth.
> Sing to the LORD, praise his name;
> proclaim his salvation day after day.
> Declare his glory among the nations,
> his marvelous deeds among all peoples.
>
> For great is the LORD and most worthy of praise;
> he is to be feared above all gods.
> For all the gods of the nations are idols,
> but the LORD made the heavens.
> Splendor and majesty are before him;
> strength and glory are in his sanctuary.

Ascribe to the LORD, O families of nations,
ascribe to the LORD glory and strength.
Ascribe to the LORD the glory due his name;
bring an offering and come into his courts.
Worship the LORD in the splendor of his holiness;
tremble before him, all the earth.

Say among the nations, "The LORD reigns."
The world is firmly established, it cannot be moved;
he will judge the peoples with equity.
Let the heavens rejoice, let the earth be glad;
let the sea resound, and all that is in it;
let the fields be jubilant, and everything in them.
Then all the trees of the forest will sing for joy;
they will sing before the LORD, for he comes,
he comes to judge the earth.
He will judge the world in righteousness
and the peoples in his truth.

—Psalm 96

Put into practice the teaching of 1 John 4 as you examine some of the different messages of Christianity you see or hear today.

ADDITIONAL RESOURCES

BOOKS

▸ Barron, Bruce. *The Health and Wealth Gospel.* Downers Grove, Ill.: InterVarsity Press, 1987.

▸ Edwards, Jonathan. *A Faithful Narrative of the Surprising Work of God.* Grand Rapids, Mich.: Baker Book House, 1979.

▸ Gaffin, Jr., Richard B. *Perspectives on Pentecost: New Testament Teaching on the Gifts of the Holy Spirit.* Phillipsburg, N.J.: Presbyterian & Reformed Publishing Co., 1979.

▸ Warfield, Benjamin B. *Counterfeit Miracles.* London: The Banner of Truth Trust, 1972.

CHAPTER ELEVEN

PERSONAL AND CONGREGATIONAL APPLICATION

BEAMS OF HEAVEN, AS I GO
THROUGH THIS WILDERNESS BELOW,
GUIDE MY FEET IN PEACEFUL WAYS,
TURN MY MIDNIGHTS INTO DAYS;
WHEN IN THE DARKNESS I WOULD GROPE,
FAITH ALWAYS SEES A STAR OF HOPE,
AND SOON FROM ALL LIFE'S GRIEF AND DANGER,
I SHALL BE FREE SOME DAY.

I DO NOT KNOW HOW LONG 'TWILL BE,
NOR WHAT THE FUTURE HOLDS FOR ME,
BUT THIS I KNOW, IF JESUS LEADS ME,
I SHALL GET HOME SOME DAY.

HARDER YET MAY BE THE FIGHT,
RIGHT MAY OFTEN YIELD TO MIGHT,
WICKEDNESS A-WHILE MAY REIGN,
SATAN'S CAUSE MAY SEEM TO GAIN;
THERE IS A GOD THAT RULES ABOVE,
WITH HAND OF POW'R AND HEART OF LOVE,
IF I AM RIGHT, HE'LL FIGHT MY BATTLE,
I SHALL HAVE PEACE SOME DAY.

—Charles A. Tindley, "Some Day," 1851-1933

Living just twelve miles from New York City, I occasionally visit the Tuesday night prayer service at Brooklyn Tabernacle. Pastor Jim Cymbala calls the Tuesday service the most important service of the week. It's amazing to see thousands of people lined up outside waiting to get into a prayer service. Once inside, people line up to be prayed for personally by the intercessors present before the service begins. Hunger for prayer and recognition of the power of prayer are evident.

This church has lived out what it means to be a praying church and has helped many to become praying people. In doing so, they have multiplied into congregations in every borough of the city; they weekly lead hundreds to Christ and see people healed and delivered.

In this chapter, we will explore what can happen when we, too, pray and work with the Lord in ministry both in our personal and congregational lives. For the personal application, we will use the story of Job to explore how spiritual battles are fought in our human lives. It will be helpful if you read or at least scan the book of Job, noticing especially

▸ Satan's conversations with God and attacks on Job (1:6-2:10).
▸ Job's relationship with God (1:1; 19:25-27).
▸ Job's testimony to God's greatness and justice (9:4-10; 12:13-25).
▸ Job's prayer for deliverance (6:8-10).
▸ Job's series of rhetorical questions (3:11-12, 16, 20-23; 10:3-10)
▸ Job's accusations (16:7-9; 23:1-5).

For the congregational application, we will first review how signs and wonders impacted the early church described in the book of Acts in these four vital areas:

▸ worship
▸ witness
▸ fellowship
▸ discipleship

Then we will take a closer look at how signs and wonders interact with these four areas in the life of the church today.

PERSONAL APPLICATION: A CASE STUDY OF JOB

Job lived his life in fellowship with God, making him part of God's kingdom. Job listened and responded to the Word of God, and it played a vital part in his life. The Holy Spirit generated faith in Job, even in the midst of questions.

The conflict between the kingdom of God and Satan is seen in Satan's testing of Job. Job was not aware of the cosmic nature of this conflict. He could only see his personal pain and questions, but by holding on to his faith in the midst of his suffering, Job defeated Satan. The attacks of the prince of this world are defeated by the miracle of faith in the midst of suffering.

Job's friends gave all the "answers" about God in neat formulas. They believed that Job's sin caused the tragedies of his life. If he confessed, he would be well. This was a typical Old Testament view of sickness. Although sin is sometimes the cause of sickness, as David testified in Psalm 32, it was not in Job's case. We see that Job was upright and believed in the power of God to restore, yet he remained in his broken condition. We see that God heard his prayer, yet did not deliver him immediately. It was Job's relationship with God that enabled him to shake his fists at God, ask God questions, and, finally, shut up before the power of the Almighty.

God does not answer Job's questions; neither does God rebuke Job for a lack of faith. Through his love and grace, God meets Job in the midst of his suffering.

The restoration of Job's health and wealth was by the grace of God, received by Job through faith, even in the midst of doubt. Job continued to pray in the midst of despair. Even though Job was unaware that he was under a satanic attack, his ability to continue living and believing in the midst of unanswered questions is a sign and wonder that led to God's defeat of Satan. It also led to the wonders of God's restoration in Job's life.

One can only speculate what might have happened if Job had taken his wife's advice to "curse God and die" (Job 2:9). Job would have missed out on the blessings of healing and restoration that God had prepared for him. In addition, Satan would have won a spiritual victory. It is ironic that it was Job's faith that led to the demonic attacks by Satan *and* to the gracious restoration by God. It is also significant that spiritual battles in the heavens are fought in the midst of the lives of ordinary people.

Sometimes I wonder if Job would have responded differently if he had known what we know now with the New Testament revelation. Would he have more readily recognized the spiritual battle with Satan? Would he have prayed differently for healing? Would he have been restored sooner if he had exhibited greater faith? Of course, we can only speculate on the answers to these questions, but often I experience Christians today who act like Job even though God has revealed so much more to us than Job ever knew.

I find the greatest revelation at the end of the book where Job recognizes that through his struggle, he has come to know God in a new way. "My ears had heard of you but now my eyes have seen you" (42:5). Although Job had been a righteous man, he was now a man who had seen God face to face. Truly, God's desire for us is that our eyes see God in the face of Jesus Christ. Only through this relationship, can we

- ▸ hear the Word of God.
- ▸ live in the presence of the kingdom of God.
- ▸ receive the power of the Holy Spirit.
- ▸ pray with power.
- ▸ grow in faith.
- ▸ defeat the devil.

The apostle Paul put it best: "For God, who said, 'Let light shine out of darkness,' made his light shine in our hearts to give us the light of the knowledge of the glory of God in the face of Christ" (2 Cor. 4:6).

Congregational Application: Then and Now

THE CHURCH IN ACTS
In this study we have often looked at texts in the book of Acts that mention signs and wonders. As we read the verses before and after these texts, we see the impact that signs and wonders had on the life of the early church. Following is a quick summary of that impact, categorized according to four vital areas in the life of the church.

WORSHIP

▶ *Praise.* "They broke bread in their homes . . . praising God" (Acts 2:46-47).
▶ *Prayer.* "They devoted themselves to . . . prayer" (2:42). "They raised their voices together in prayer to God. . . . 'Stretch out your hand to heal and perform miraculous signs and wonders'" (4:24-30).
▶ *Confession.* "When the people heard this, they were cut to the heart. . . . Those who accepted [Peter's] message [to repent] were baptized" (2:37-41).
▶ *The Lord's Supper.* "They devoted themselves to . . . the breaking of bread" (4:42).
▶ *The Word.* "They devoted themselves to the apostles teaching" (2:42). "And they were all filled with the Holy Spirit and spoke the word of God boldly" (4:31). "'The men you put in jail are . . . teaching the people'" (5:25). "So the twelve . . . said, 'It would not be right for us to neglect the ministry of the word of God" (6:2).

WITNESS

▶ *Conviction of Sin and Conversions.* "When the day of Pentecost came . . . there were staying in Jerusalem God-fearing Jews from every nation under heaven. . . . Those who accepted [Peter's] message were baptized, and about three thousand were added to their number that day" (2:1-41).
▶ *Healing, Exorcism, and Church Growth.* "The apostles performed many miraculous signs and wonders. . . . Crowds gathered also from the towns around Jerusalem, bringing their sick and those tormented by evil spirits, and all of them were healed" (5:12-16).

FELLOWSHIP

▶ *Koinonia (sharing).* "They devoted themselves to . . . fellowship" (2:42).
▶ *Caring.* "All the believers were together and had everything in common. . . . they gave to anyone as they had need. They . . . ate together . . . enjoying the favor of all the people" (2:42-47).

▸ *Leadership.* "Brothers, choose seven men from among you who are known to be full of the Spirit and wisdom" (6:3).

DISCIPLESHIP

▸ *Word and Prayer.* "They devoted themselves to the apostles' teaching and . . . to prayer" (2:42). "Day after day, in the temple courts and from house to house, they never stopped teaching and proclaiming the good news that Jesus is the Christ" (5:42).

THE CHURCH TODAY

It was over fifteen years ago that our congregation first began exploring how God wanted us to put into practice some of the principles we've discussed in this book. Because we were excited about what God was teaching us about prayer, we began training servants of prayer and holding healing services.

I still vividly remember holding three-year-old Zneida in my arms on a Sunday morning as we prayed for her. She was born with a hole in her heart and needed surgery to correct it. We prayed with boldness, persistence, faith, and in accord with the Word of God. The doctors operated, but complications set in. As though it were yesterday, I remember standing by Zneida's bedside as her heart rate dropped to nothing, and she died. Soon after that, one of our emerging leaders was diagnosed with AIDS. Again we prayed in faith, with passion, trusting in God for healing and deliverance. Within three months, he too died.

These seeming "failures" left us discouraged and with questions. What was God saying to us? Did we expect too much? Did we have too little faith? Were we trying to tell God what to do? We learned that living by faith is living with many unanswered questions, yet continuing to trust in God as Job did. We've also learned to examine the relationship between signs and wonders and our worship, witness, fellowship, and discipleship—still key elements in the life of the church today as they were for the early church.

WORSHIP

The word *worship* comes from the Hebrew word *shadah*, literally meaning "to bow down or lay out on your face." The Greek word *proshueneo* means to do obeisance, such as one would do when kneeling down to kiss the hand of a king. Our English word comes from the old English *worthship* and denotes the worthiness of the one receiving special honor.

True worship is directed toward God and involves every part of us: mind, body, soul, emotions, and intellect. It can be described as dialogue between God and his people. Worship includes praise, prayer, confession, the Word, and sacraments. Worship takes the form of praise, thanksgiving, confession, assurance, dedication, intercession, proclamation, recommitment, and confrontation. It is done individually and corporately.

We must continually be called back to biblical practices in worship, including the principles surrounding signs and wonders. Worship is a celebration of the presence of the kingdom of God now and of the future hope of Jesus' return to complete that kingdom. Worship is empowered by the indwelling Holy Spirit in all believers. Worship is a time for corporate prayers of praise, confession, intercession, and thanksgiving. Worship is a time to grow in faith and to confront the enemy and his hosts. But most of all, we can have no part in the work of God if we are not living a life of worship. Let's examine these four dimensions of worship as they relate to signs and wonders:

▶ praise
▶ prayer
▶ confession
▶ the Word of God

PRAISE

When I was growing up, we began every worship service with a psalm or hymn of praise. Usually these were considered "preliminaries"—something to fill time before hearing God's Word. For years, I missed the privilege of praise and the power of praise as a vital element of worship in which God is magnified for who he is.

The Scriptures describe numerous acts of praise. For example,

▶ at the dedication of the temple, countless singers, musicians, and priests led the people in praising God (2 Chron. 5:12-14).
▶ King Jehoshaphat, in the midst of overwhelming battle odds, marched his army into battle praising God and won the victory (2 Chron. 20:21-27).
▶ Paul and Silas were beaten and chained in prison in Philippi, but they praised God and were set free (Acts 16:22-26).

The Psalms call us over and over to praise the Lord with instruments, hand-clapping, hand-raising, dancing, and shouting. We express our love for God, and God responds.

Our praise to God sets us free from the shackles that bind us and the enemies that attack us. John Dawson, in his book *Taking Our Cities for God* (Creation House, 1989, p. 167) gives us the key for winning:

> Do you want revival in your city? Do you want to defeat the powers of darkness? The way to get rid of darkness is to turn on the light, to establish the Lord's presence in the midst of his people through praise (see Ps. 22:3).

PRAYER

Prayer is one of the most important and most neglected parts of the life of many congregations. It is a mystery of God's grace that God's kingdom here on earth is expanded and Satan defeated through the prayers of God's people.

I grew up singing the words "prayer is the Christian's vital breath" (from the hymn "Prayer Is the Soul's Sincere Desire," William H. Havergal, 1846). But is it? And do we live like it is? Prayer should be the foundation of every aspect of the life of the church.

Prayers for healing from spiritual, physical, relational, psychological, or demonic afflictions are finding their place in the life of many churches. This can be done in a variety of ways. Special worship services for Christian healing offer an opportunity to seek God's healing in our lives or in the life of a loved one. Such services usually include a time of praise, confession, assurance, and a message from God's Word related to Christian healing. Elders or trained prayer teams are then available to pray for needs. The emphasis is on believers as the body of Christ praying for one another. Oil and laying on of hands may be used.

In accord with James 5, prayer teams can meet with people requesting prayers at church or in their homes; they can be available every Sunday for those at worship. Again, the focus is not on the person praying but on Jesus Christ, our healer. Prayer team members should be properly trained to help them avoid the extremes of "pessimistic un-expectancy" or "faith-formula declarations."

Not only does prayer change things, but prayer also changes us. Our prayers for our families, congregations, neighborhoods, nations, and world will affect our relationships with and attitudes toward them. Many resources are now available from congregational and denominational sources. The Concert of Prayer movement, founded by David Bryant, also gives leadership in this area. Bryant's book, *Concerts of Prayer* (Regal Books, 1984), gives specific guidelines for carrying out a prayer ministry.

CONFESSION

Another element of worship related to God's demonstration of signs and wonders is confession. After Peter's sermon on Pentecost the people were "cut to the heart" and asked, "'What shall we do?'" (Acts 2:37).

Worship must include a "cutting to the heart" that leads to personal and corporate confession of sin. The liturgical response "Lord, have mercy" has been used for centuries. Reformed worship includes the service of confession and assurance, but we must ask if these means are leading people to heartfelt confession. It is all too easy to read through a form or sit through a prayer without really confessing our sin. As a pastor, I continually struggle with how best to help our congregation confess their sins to the Lord. Recently we have been inviting people to kneel at their pew, in the aisle, or up front. Somehow kneeling helps us to humble ourselves into a posture for confession.

In his classic work on revival, Richard Lovelace identifies "awareness of the depth of sin in yourself and the world" as one of the preconditions of renewal (*Renewal as a Way of Life*, InterVarsity Press, 1985, p. 162). Periods of revival and renewal in the church were marked by corporate outpourings of confession, as can be seen from some of the testimonies included in this book. Along with confession of individual sins, we must confess shared sins such as materialism, racism, and greed. This confession is foundational for any signs and wonders to happen related to structural and societal change.

THE WORD OF GOD

The dynamic proclamation of the Word of God is vital to the life of the church. Biblical preaching proclaims the Word and will of God. Along with the sacraments, pure preaching of the Word is seen as one of the marks of the true church in the Reformed confessions. This is preaching which arises from Scripture and is inspired by the Holy Spirit.

True preaching demands a response. It may be accompanied or followed by signs and wonders, as we saw in chapter 4. When the Word of God is preached,

- sin will be exposed.
- sinners will repent.
- those struggling will be empowered.
- those tempted will become obedient.
- the unsaved will be converted.

Following the ministry of the Word, opportunity should be given for both immediate and long-term responses to the Word. This could be in the form of an altar call following the sermon or an invitation to come to a prayer room after the service.

We see in the New Testament that God also spoke through prophesies, words of wisdom, words of knowledge, and even through the interpretation of tongues. When our church commissions new servants of prayer, we read from 1 Corinthians 12 about spiritual gifts, lay hands on them, anoint them with oil in the name of the Lord, and pray for the activation of spiritual gifts to equip them to minister to others at an upcoming healing service. All these are ongoing ways that God speaks and reveals his Word today.

WITNESS

In Jesus' last words to his disciples he tells them, "You will receive power when the Holy Spirit comes on you; and you will be my witnesses . . ." (Acts 1:8).

Harry S. Boer, a former Christian Reformed missionary, dedicated his life to this mission. His classic book *Pentecost and Missions* (Eerdmans, 1964) outlines how the spontaneous response of the "power of the Holy Spirit" on the early Christians was mission. It was not because of duty that they were witnesses, but because of the joy of their new life in Christ.

This renewal of our love for God and thanksgiving for his love for us is at the core of the witness of the church. The good news must be "good" to the one telling it if it is to have credibility. This demands knowledge of the gospel and an experience with the Lord Jesus. Through the power of the Holy Spirit working in the bearers, the gospel will go forth.

The role of the Holy Spirit is fundamental if signs and wonders are to serve an evangelistic purpose. John Wimber, in his book *Power Evangelism* (Harper and Row, 1986), calls for "power evangelism" to complement the "program evangelism" that already exists. Program evangelism can get so caught up in activities, plans, and strategies that we forget it's God's work.

Jesus told us in his great commission to teach "them to obey everything that I have commanded you" (Matt. 28:20). For too long, we've left out of this commission Jesus' command to "drive out evil spirits and heal every disease and sickness" (10:1). Mark's version of the great commission states this more directly:

> And these signs will accompany those who believe: In my name they will drive out demons; they will speak in new tongues; they will pick up snakes with their hands; and when they drink deadly poison, it will not hurt them at all; they will place their hands on sick people, and they will get well.
>
> —Mark 16:17-18

Although we don't need to go out looking for snakes or drinking poison, we should witness, expecting the signs that Jesus promised us.

FELLOWSHIP

Fellowship in the life of the church finds its meaning from the Greek word *koinonia*. Much more than social activities, it incorporates the meaning of "communion, close relationship, gift usage, generosity, participation, and sharing" (Walter Bauer, *A Greek-English Lexicon of the New Testament,* University of Chicago Press, 1957, pp. 439-440). This represents the real life of any congregation. As a result of fellowship in the early church, the believers "gave to anyone as he had need" and enjoyed "the favor of all the people" (Acts 2:45, 47).

Fellowship includes applying the principles we've discussed to every aspect of our congregational life together. Specifically related to spiritual gifts, it means recognizing and using all the gifts of the Holy Spirit to build up the body of Christ. These are especially important in our care for one another. When, in the life of the church, we can lay hands on each other and pray for each other, the body is strengthened. When we are able to give or receive a word of knowledge or wisdom from someone in our community, fellowship with each other is deepened. When we join together in God's mission, our sense of purpose and calling will be expanded.

Racial, cultural, economic, and class differences often form barriers within congregations. These differences must not be ignored or denied but faced squarely and addressed in Christian love. Such differences affect how we minister to one another and those around us.

DISCIPLESHIP

The principles in this book find new application in the area of discipleship, especially in regard to spiritual warfare, prayer, spiritual gifts, and faith. Although in Reformed circles we have always stressed the Word of God, the danger is that this emphasis leads to more biblical and doctrinal knowledge than real discipleship. Discipleship is *following* Jesus— not just knowing about Jesus.

Jesus used the most basic method of training: I do it; you watch me; we do it together. You do it; I watch you; we do it together; somebody else watches us. Out of this model of discipleship, the church grew from 120 members before Pentecost to over 30 million in 300 years.

It is imperative that we disciple new believers in the ways of the Holy Spirit. For example, although the confessions of my own denomination include teaching about the personal attacks of the devil, I was never taught how to do spiritual warfare. We must not be preoccupied with Satan, but neither can we pretend that he does exist. Doing so will leave us powerless in the conflicts where we do not even recognize the enemy. Early baptism liturgies (see "Instructions Regarding Baptism" later in this chapter) included the casting out of any evil spirit to make room for the Holy Spirit. In light of the spiritual warfare we face, it may be time to examine our own liturgical forms.

We can learn from the African church. A former Christian Reformed missionary to Africa, Hank Pott identifies warfare as one of four parts of a healthy church.

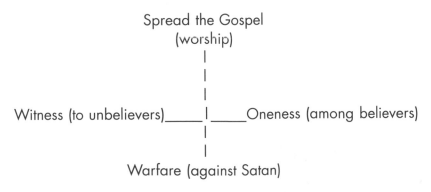

Spread the Gospel
(worship)
|
|
|
Witness (to unbelievers)_____|_____Oneness (among believers)
|
|
Warfare (against Satan)

—"Lessons from Africa Warfare," *The Banner,* June 8, 1987, p. 10.

Another manifestation of signs and wonders related to discipleship is living a life of holiness and obedience. The Heidelberg Catechism's placement of the Ten Commandments in the section on gratitude is an example of the Reformed emphasis. Out of thanksgiving for the grace of God, Christians are to live a life of obedient gratitude.

The Reformed faith has often emphasized what Christians should *not* do to live a life of holiness: do not kill, lie, steal, commit adultery, covet— the list goes on. This is good advice, since it comes from God himself, but we have often neglected to emphasize some of the things that we *should* do. Jesus' last words were for us to "go and make disciples of all nations, baptizing them . . . and teaching them to obey all that I have command- ed you" (Matt. 28:19-20). The Christian church as a whole has not been faithful to teach obedience to all that Jesus commanded us. In fact, many call this the great *omission* of the great commission.

It is only out of a transformed Christian life lived in relationship with Christ that we can be all that God wants us to be. This calls for a life of discipleship lived out in community with each other. In his profound work on discipleship, Dallas Willard says the church is so spiritually weak today because "they have failed to seek his power to the ends he speci- fied, and they have not developed the character needed to bear his power safely throughout the social order, or even within the church itself" (*The Spirit of the Disciplines,* InterVarsity Press, 1988, p. 246).

The vision of our church is to see our community "transformed by the power of Jesus." This includes transformation of individuals and families who are part of our congregation and community. It is our desire to see the community *become* the congregation. Every week our bulletin invites people at the conclusion of the service for prayer and anointing with oil for spiritual, physical, emotional, and relational healing in their lives. As this happens both in the church and on the street, we see this vision tak- ing place. We see the signs and wonders of God as

▸ men and women come to Christ and are saved.
▸ residents in our Discipleship House are delivered from years of drug addiction.
▸ physical illnesses are healed.
▸ marriages are restored.
▸ demonic attacks on leaders are repealed.
▸ high praise is offered to God.
▸ spiritual gifts are released.
▸ hunger for God increases.
▸ real community and fellowship happens.

Although it is always God who does the miracle or sign and wonder, the Lord invites us to engage with him in these acts of power. As we put ourselves in positions and places to proclaim the Word of God and the kingdom of God, to be filled with the Holy Spirit, to pray with power, and to believe in faith, we will see the Lord work signs and wonders to defeat the devil and bring God glory. Although the Lord works in us individually, we are always called to function in Christian community as the body of Christ.

TESTIMONIES FROM . . .

INSTRUCTIONS REGARDING BAPTISM FROM THE APOSTOLIC TRADITION OF HIPPOLYTUS (A.D. 200)

Let them who will be baptized fast on the preparation of the Sabbath (Friday). And on the Sabbath (Saturday) when they who will be baptized have assembled in one place by the direction of the bishop, let them all be commanded to pray and bend their knees. And when he has laid his hand upon them, let him exorcize all alien spirits to flee from them, and not to return to them henceforward. And when he has done exorcizing, let him breathe in their face. And when he has sealed their foreheads and their ears and their noses, let him raise them up. And let them spend all the night in vigil, and let them be read to and instructed.

And at the hour which is determined for baptizing, let the bishop give thanks over the oil, and put it into a vessel, and call it oil of the thanksgiving, and take also other oil, and exorcize (upon) it and call it the oil of exorcism. And a deacon should carry the oil of exorcism and stand on the left hand of the presbyter, and another deacon shall take the oil of the thanksgiving and stand on the right hand of the presbyter. And when the presbyter has taken hold of each one of those who will be baptized, let him command him to renounce, saying, "I renounce thee, Satan, and all thy service and all thy works." And when he has renounced all these, let him anoint him with the oil of exorcism, saying, "Let all spirits remove far from thee." And then let him give him to the bishop naked, or to the presbyter who stands at the water for baptizing.

—Henry Ansgar Kelly, *The Devil at Baptism: Ritual, Theology and Drama*, Cornell University Press, 1985, pp. 84, 89.

MARTIN LUTHER (1500s)

The tax collector in Torgau and the councilor in Belgern have written me to ask that I offer some good advice and help for Mrs. John Korner's afflicted husband. I know of no worldly help to give. If the physicians are at a loss to find a remedy, you may be sure that it is not a case of ordinary melancholy. It must, rather, be an affliction that comes from the devil, and this must be counteracted by the power of Christ and the prayer of faith. . . . Accordingly, you should proceed as follows: Go to him with the deacon and two or three good men. Confident that you, as pastor of the place, are clothed with the authority of the ministerial office, lay your hands upon him and say, "Peace be with you, dear brother, from God our Father and from our Lord Jesus Christ." Thereupon, repeat the Creed and the Lord's Prayer over him in a clear voice and close with these words: "O God, almighty Father, who has told us through thy Son, 'Verily, verily I say unto you, Whatsoever ye shall ask the Father in my name, he will give it you,' who has commanded and encouraged us to pray in his name, 'Ask and ye shall receive' and who in like manner hast said, 'Call upon me in the day of trouble: I will deliver thee, and thou shalt glorify me,' we unworthy sinners, relying on these thy words and commands, pray for thy mercy with such faith as we can muster. Graciously deign to free this man from all evil, and put to naught the work that Satan has done in him, to the honor of thy name and the strengthening of the faith of believers; through the same Jesus Christ, thy Son, our Lord, who liveth and reigneth with thee, world without end. Amen." Then, when you depart, lay your hands upon the man again and say, "These signs shall follow them that believe; they shall lay hands on the sick, and they shall recover." Do this three times, once on each of three successive days.

—*Letters of Spiritual Council*, Library of Christian Classics, Tappert Edition, Westminster Press, Vol. 18, p. 52.

JONATHAN EDWARDS (1735)

This work of God, as it was carried on, and the number of true saints multiplied, soon made a glorious alteration in the town; so that in the spring and summer following 1735, the town seemed to be full of the presence of God; it never was so full of love, nor so full of joy, and yet so full of distress as it was then. There were remarkable tokens of God's presence in almost every house. It was a time of joy in families on account of salvation being brought to them; parents rejoicing over their children as new born, and husbands over their wives, and wives over their husbands. The doings of God were then seen in his sanctuary, God's day was a delight, and his tabernacles were amiable. Our public assemblies were then beautiful; the congregation was alive in God's service, every one earnestly intent on the public worship, every hearer eager to drink in the words of the minister as they came from his mouth; the assembly in general were, from time to time, in tears while the word was preached; some weeping with sorrow and distress, others with joy and love, others with pity and concern for the souls of their neighbors. Our public praises were then greatly enlivened.

—*A Faithful Narrative of the Surprising Work of God,*
Baker Book House, 1979, pp. 16-17.

KRIENGSAK CHAREONWONGSAK (1990)

At the Hope of Bangkok [Thailand] Church, members are encouraged to allow the Holy Spirit to guide them during worship and their daily lives to express their love and gratitude to God. Spontaneous worship and orderly functioning of the gifts of the Holy Spirit have drawn members closer to God. Signs and wonders are performed by the Holy Spirit, especially through members laying hands on one another in prayer. These experiences confirm in people's hearts that God is powerful and still free to work today. In a country where even nonbelievers believe in miracles by supernatural power, signs and wonders through the God of the Bible have partially contributed to the significant growth of this church. This is reflected in the innumerable verifiable testimonies that members share about God's healing power and answered prayers. The joyful, expressive, lively, contagious, victorious praise and celebration in our worship services is an important aspect of the Hope of Bangkok. They remind people that God is alive and in our midst. For fun-loving Thais, this has added to the "fun" of coming to church. God loves his people to rejoice before him, and so do we.

—"Hope of Bangkok: A Visionary Model of Church Growth and Church Planting," *Urban Mission,* 1990, Vol. 7:3, pp. 25-35.

Reformed Reflections

THE HEIDELBERG CATECHISM, Q&A 1

**Q. What is your only comfort
in life and in death?**

A. That I am not my own,
but belong—
  body and soul,
  in life and in death—
to my faithful Savior Jesus Christ.

  He has fully paid for all my sins with his precious blood,
  and has set me free from the tyranny of the devil.
  He also watches over me in such a way
  that not a hair can fall from my head
  without the will of my Father in heaven;
  in fact, all things must work together for my salvation.

Because I belong to him,
Christ, by his Holy Spirit,
assures me of eternal life
and makes me wholeheartedly willing and ready
from now on to live for him.

Reflect on how belonging to Christ sets you
"free from the tyranny of the devil." Be specific.

OUR WORLD BELONGS TO GOD: A CONTEMPORARY TESTIMONY, STANZAS 37 AND 39

In our world, bent under the weight of sin,
Christ gathers a new community.
Satan and his evil forces
seek whom they may confuse and swallow;
but Jesus builds his church,
his Spirit guides,
and grace abounds.

Our new life in Christ
is celebrated and nourished
in the fellowship of congregations
where God's name is praised
his Word proclaimed,
his way taught;
where sins are confessed,
prayers and gifts are offered,
and sacraments are celebrated.

Reflect on how your church lives out this confession together.

QUESTIONS TO THINK ABOUT
▸ How are you growing as a disciple of Christ, learning to "obey every-thing" he commanded?
▸ What do you think God wants you to learn about signs and wonders personally and in your church?
▸ How does your church compare to the Acts 2 church?
▸ How does your church measure up to the four parts of a healthy church in Africa?
▸ What characteristics of spiritual renewal are evident in your congregation?
▸ What are some barriers or roadblocks that hinder congregational renewal?
▸ How can your congregation apply some of the principles discussed in this book?

PRAYER AND PRACTICE
Pray this conclusion to the believer's prayer:

Now, Lord,
consider their threats and enable your servants
to speak your word with great boldness.
Stretch out your hand
to heal and perform miraculous signs and wonders
through the name of your holy servant Jesus.

—Acts 4:29-30

This week, obey Jesus' command to heal the sick with someone who tells you about their sickness. Don't just promise to pray for them. Instead, right then and there, ask if you can pray for them. Then pray for Jesus to heal them. If you don't meet any sick people, pray in response to any need that someone tells you about. Ask caringly, "May I pray for you about that right now?" You'll have a divine opportunity to minister.

ADDITIONAL RESOURCES

BOOKS
▸ Bryant, David. *Concerts of Prayer*. Ventura, Calif.: Regal Books, 1984.
▸ Dawson, John. *Taking Our Cities for God*. Lake Mary, Fla: Creation House, 1989.
▸ Lawrence, Roy. *Christian Healing Rediscovered*. Downers Grove, Ill.: InterVarsity Press, 1980.

TRAINING RESOURCES
The Dunamis Project. Presbyterian-Reformed Ministries International, www.prmi.org. A series of six workshops/seminars taught in a weekend or week-long session:

I. Gateways to Empowered Ministry
II. In the Spirit's Power
III. The Power of Prayer
IV. The Healing Ministry of Jesus
V. Equipping for Spiritual Warfare
VI. Mission and Evangelism

Priddy, Kenneth E., and J. Patrick Bragg, Jr. *Project 6:15—A Two-Year Commitment to Church Redevelopment That Combines Spiritual Renewal with Strategic Initiative*. Richmond, Va.: United Front Ministries, 2003. www.unitedfrontministries.com.

VIDEOS/DVDS:
▸ Otis Jr., George. *The Quickening: Entering into the Firestorm of God's Grace*. The Sentinel Group, Global Net Productions, 2003. www.transformnations.com.

▶ ————. *Transformations*. The Sentinel Group, Global Net Productions, 1999.

▶ ————. *Transformations II*. The Sentinel Group, Global Net Productions, 2001.

CHAPTER 12

SOCIETAL AND STRUCTURAL APPLICATION

LEAD ON, O KING ETERNAL,
THE DAY OF MARCH HAS COME;
HENCEFORTH IN FIELDS OF CONQUEST
YOUR TENTS WILL BE OUR HOME.
THROUGH DAYS OF PREPARATION
YOUR GRACE HAS MADE US STRONG;
AND NOW, O KING ETERNAL,
WE LIFT OUR BATTLE SONG.

LEAD ON, O KING ETERNAL,
TILL SIN'S FIERCE WAR SHALL CEASE,
AND HOLINESS SHALL WHISPER
THE SWEET AMEN OF PEACE.
FOR NOT WITH SWORD'S LOUD CLASHING
OR ROLL OF STIRRING DRUMS—
WITH DEEDS OF LOVE AND MERCY
THE HEAVENLY KINGDOM COMES.

LEAD ON, O KING ETERNAL;
WE FOLLOW, NOT WITH FEARS,
FOR GLADNESS BREAKS LIKE MORNING
WHERE'ER YOUR FACE APPEARS.
YOUR CROSS IS LIFTED O'ER US,
WE JOURNEY IN ITS LIGHT;
THE CROWN AWAITS THE CONQUEST;
LEAD ON, O GOD OF MIGHT.

—Ernest W. Shurtleff, 1888 alt.

I recently watched a PBS special on slavery in America. It portrayed the horrific nature of American slavery compared to slavery throughout history in other nations. In America, the separation of families, breeding, and intentional strategies of total control and dehumanization were common—and practiced by those who called themselves Christians. Even Jonathan Edwards, the Reformed preacher of the Great Awakening, owned slaves. How can it be that people who follow Jesus are very aware of certain personal sins but blind to others?

The unconfessed sin of racism has plagued the church through the ages, and continues to raise its ugly head. In this final chapter, we will examine how racism and other power structures have impacted society throughout the ages. We will

▸ identify the systems and structures of societies.
▸ describe structural change during Bible times.
▸ examine the process of confrontation today while looking back over church history.
▸ contrast the evangelical and Reformed views on personal and structural change.
▸ apply the principles we've discussed about signs and wonders to the Christian's role in confronting these powers to bring societal and structural change in the name of Christ.

IDENTIFYING THE SYSTEMS AND STRUCTURES OF SOCIETY

The apostle Paul uses four different terms to describe the systems and structures of nations and societies. These are described together in Colossians 1:16 as "thrones or powers or rulers or authorities" and in Ephesians 6:12 as "the rulers . . . the authorities . . . the powers of this dark world and . . . the spiritual forces of evil in the heavenly realms."

These power structures were created by God and can be used for good or for evil. They include education, the military, family, church, economics, the arts, science, technology, race, government, and religion. They were corrupted in the Fall, but through Christ's redemption they can be reclaimed.

These powers are more than fallen structures because of the sinful people who run them. They take on a life of their own that makes them superhuman and capable of being possessed, influenced, and directed by supernatural evil spirits.

Structural Change in Bible Times

STRUCTURAL CHANGE IN THE OLD TESTAMENT

In the Old Testament, signs and wonders yielded both personal change and national and structural change in political, economic, and social areas. Proof of this change is evident in these familiar events:

▸ The ungodliness of early civilizations led to the flood, and then to a new civilization through Noah and his family (Gen. 6:5-8).
▸ The pride of the people who built the tower of Babel led God to confuse their languages and scatter them into many nations (Gen. 11).
▸ The wickedness of the inhabitants of Sodom and Gomorrah led to the destruction of the entire social, political, and economic life of those cities (Gen. 18-19).
▸ God's revelation to Joseph of Pharaoh's dreams led Joseph to the height of Egyptian political and economic power (Gen. 41). Later, Egypt's oppression of the Israelites led to God's deliverance of Israel and the destruction of Egypt's military might (Ex. 4-15).

During the time of the judges we see God working through Gideon, Deborah, Samson, and others. During the times of the kings we see the miracles of Elijah and Elisha. The prophets were advocates of God's justice and gave hope of God's future shalom. They called the people to personal repentance; they called them to end the oppression of the poor and to discontinue the corruption and injustice that they practiced. These sins led to the destruction of the kingdoms of Israel and Judah.

When God revealed the meaning of Nebuchadnezzar's dreams to Daniel, he and his friends were placed in positions of political influence and power (Dan. 2). Later, Shadrach, Meshach, and Abednego refused to bow to an idol and were thrown into the fiery furnace but were not harmed. As a result, Nebuchadnezzar praised Yahweh and called on all the people to recognize this powerful God in Babylon (Dan. 3). Under Persian rule, Daniel refused to worship the king but continued to worship

Yahweh (Dan. 4). After God delivered Daniel from the lions' den, Darius, emperor of Persia, decreed that all people of his empire must fear the God of Daniel.

In the Old Testament, God works through signs and wonders, but more often God works through people like you and like me. Either way, a close link between salvation and social, economic, and political issues exists throughout the Old Testament.

STRUCTURAL CHANGE IN THE NEW TESTAMENT

In the New Testament, Jesus was undaunted by the religious and political leaders of his day. He let them know that they had no power over him. Jesus reminded Pilate that any authority he had was from God himself: "You would have no power over me it were it not given to you from above" (John 19:11).

▸ Through his death, Jesus conquered the "powers and authorities" (Col. 2:15).
▸ Through his resurrection, Jesus embarrassed political and religious leaders, threatening the status quo (Matt. 28:11-15).
▸ Through his ascension, Jesus showed that all power belongs to him (Phil. 2:9-11).

The signs and wonders done by the apostles also brought about structural and societal change. In Saul's conversion, the power of religious persecution was broken, and he became one of the first world missionaries (Acts 9). The deliverance from prison of Peter (Acts 12) and Paul and Silas (Acts 16) led to the humbling of political and military powers. In spite of persecution, the church continued to grow and the Word of God spread.

Some of these events brought about permanent political and social change. Others were eschatological reminders of who is in control and what God's will is for the way people are to treat each other. Jesus expanded "your neighbor" in Leviticus 19:18 to include not only those like ourselves but also those whom we would least expect to help us, and those of other ethnic groups (Luke 10:29-37). In his summary of the law (Matt. 22:35-40), Jesus put a person's relationship to his neighbor on the same level as his or her relationship to God.

According to Jesus' words in Luke 4:18-21, loving one's neighbor means to

- preach good news to the poor.
- proclaim freedom for the prisoners and recovery of sight for the blind.
- release the oppressed.
- proclaim the year of the Lord's favor.

When Jesus comes again, he will make all things new and usher in the New Jerusalem described in Revelation 21.

CONFRONTING THE POWERS

Recognizing the spiritual dimension of the powers is the first step toward confronting them. This calls for first naming the demons and then casting them out of social structures. Like any exorcism, this spiritual battle requires the sovereignty of Almighty God, the victory of Christ, and the power of the Holy Spirit. Richard R. Lovelace cautions,

> Structural exorcism is real spiritual warfare which requires more than theorizing, demonstrating, legislating, making pronouncements, and other conventional modes of social action. It may require all of these. But it also requires comprehensive spiritual renewal through the strength available in Christ. And especially it requires the exercise of prayer.
> —*Dynamics of Spiritual Life,* InterVarsity Press, 1979, p. 385.

Robert Linthicum identifies the city as a primary battlefield between God and Satan because it is in the city that the powers are concentrated. He says,

> We can discern Satan's urban strategy. He seeks to capture the soul of a city through the seduction of its systems and structures. In that seduction, he uses the principalities and powers (the spiritual dimensions of the systems). By seducing the systems, Satan shapes the conditions of the city's formal and informal groups, families, and the lives of individuals so that he can seduce the people as well. Whenever he is successful in seducing systems or people by means of the principalities and powers, Satan is able to shape profoundly the interior spirituality (brooding angel) of that city and the rest of its institutions.
> —*City of God—City of Satan: A Biblical Theology of the Urban Church,* Zondervan Publishing House, 1991, p. 77.

Discerning Satan's urban strategy is easier said than done. In 1978 I and other clergy of the Paterson Clergy Association attempted to minister to the troubled Paterson educational system by exorcising its demons and redeeming it in the name of Christ. But more than 25 years later, the educational system is still in trouble. Many of the demons still exist, and many of our children are failing. We have not seen the kind of transformation for which we have prayed and hoped. Obviously, we have a lot to learn about this important ministry. Did we fail to identify the demons? Did we fail to confront them effectively?

In two *Transformations* videos produced in 1999 and 2001 (see "Additional Resources" in chapter 11), George Otis Jr. of the Sentinel Group documents strategies and victories over demonic political systems in several nations around the world. In 2003, he produced *The Quickening: Entering into the Firestorm of God's Grace* (Sentinel Group, Global Net Productions), a video that identifies these seven principles for realizing community transformation:

▸ God wants to be invited into our communities.
▸ God is drawn to holiness and humility.
▸ Corporate revival begins with individual obedience.
▸ Biblical unity is a majority with God.
▸ Breakthrough prayer releases destiny.
▸ God's work will always be unique.
▸ God uses servant leaders who will persevere through struggle and opposition.

LESSONS FROM CHURCH HISTORY

When thinking about how to confront the powers today, it is helpful to look at how this has been done throughout church history. Greek philosophical thought separated the body and soul and elevated the mind and soul over the body, leading to the influence of Gnosticism in the church. That dichotomy between soul and body, word and deed, evangelism and social justice, proclamation and demonstration, personal transformation and corporate change, has distorted the truth of the gospel.

Throughout church history, individuals tried to confront the structural powers of their day in many different ways. Consider these examples:

In the fourth century, Constantine sought to Christianize the "powers" by establishing the Holy Roman Empire as a result of his own encounter with Christ. Unfortunately, the church and the empire became hopelessly intertwined in destructive ways for a thousand years.

Out of the Protestant Reformation, John Calvin established the city of Geneva as a theocracy where every structure of the city—education, economics, politics, and other social structures—would be a witness for Christ. It's ironic that both Constantine and Calvin used coercion to establish these representations of the kingdom of God.

The Puritan Cotton Mather also sought this goal of establishing a Christian society in New England.

In the late nineteenth century Netherlands, a movement called Neo-Calvinism led by Abraham Kuyper sought to recapture the Reformation emphasis on the lordship of Christ over all of creation. One of his most famous quotes is: "There is not one square inch of the universe that is not under the lordship of Jesus Christ."

During the first half of the twentieth century, a separation developed between evangelism and social concern in the church in the United States. Evangelicals recognized the need for individuals to be "born again" (to have a personal power encounter with the living God) but missed the need for structures to also be "born again." Closely aligned with fundamentalism was the growth of dispensational theology, which affected Christian views about the presence of the kingdom of God and discouraged involvement in social and structural concerns.

At the other extreme, some of the streams of Christianity that stressed the social nature of the gospel became more liberal related to the authority of Scripture and salvation by faith alone in Jesus Christ. This has been expressed in the "social gospel" as well as in elements of liberation theology.

The African American church in the United States is an excellent example of integrating the gospel in addressing personal and social needs. The church spoke prophetically and powerfully about what it means to be created in the image of God. This led to tremendous oppression, persecution, and martyrdom, much like the prophets of the Old Testament suffered, but it also led to positive steps forward in civil rights. The battle is surely not over—racism is still alive and well—but we see that change is possible through the power of the gospel.

Power Encounter: Personal and Structural Change

With this brief historical review as background, let's continue to explore how structural change is to be accomplished.

Some have divorced Christianity from social concern in the hope that conversion of souls will trickle down into transformation of structures. The opposite extreme seeks the transformation of systems and structures through liberation from injustice and oppression but misses the need to be personally born again of the Spirit of God. Both these positions are a distortion of the gospel.

The Reformed position recognizes the need for personal salvation but also for structural salvation. Yet both the evangelical position, which focuses on individual change, and the Reformed position have often overlooked the real demonic nature of structural powers. Let's focus now on contrasting these two positions in an attempt to arrive at a specific strategy of application.

EVANGELICAL INDIVIDUALISM

A well-known contemporary evangelical position is to change corrupt structures by changing the people who run those structures. John Wimber, one of the founders of the signs and wonders movement, has healed thousands of diseases but does not apply these powerful truths structurally.

> I do not think we are to use political or economic means to change society. If you want to strike a blow against abortion, win an abortionist to Christ. If you're against drug abuse, win a drug dealer to Christ. If you don't like crooked politics, win a politician to Christ. Our means—as we've been commissioned by Christ—is to lead men to him.
>
> —*Power Evangelism*, Harper & Row, 1986, p. 12.

Harvie Conn, in his book *A Clarified Vision for Urban Mission* (Zondervan, 1987, p. 129), terms this "The Privatization Generalization." He states,

> The church has clung to a private, individualistic notion of sin. . . . Social structures, as instruments of human interaction, are seen as sinful only in terms of the individuals who constitute them. Their holistic character, long an object of study for soci-

ology and cultural anthropology, loses integrity under the force of individualistic compartmentalization.

Ideally, every Christian should be working to establish the kingdom of God in complete justice and righteousness in all areas of life. But reality is often different. Tom Skinner, former Harlem gang leader turned evangelist, observes,

> African Americans don't believe that white Christians who love Jesus act any differently towards them than do white people who don't love Jesus. . . . White American Christians are more committed to America and the American dream than they are to the kingdom of God.
> —"Racism Still Divides Black and White America,"
> *Public Justice Report*, Vol.14, No.8, May-June, 1991, p.4.

Skinner's statement is never more evident than in the history of the Pentecostal church in America. This is usually traced to the 1906 Azusa Street Revival, birthed out of the preaching of William J. Seymour, an African American preacher. The revival grew as people of all races, including African American, Caucasian, Hispanic, Native American, and Asian, came to the Lord. Sadly, this multiracial reflection of the kingdom of God did not continue. Charles Fox Parham, the leading white pastor of the movement, was a known supporter of the Ku Klux Klan and saw race mixing as the great sin of America. Instead of a multiracial Pentecostal church giving a prophetic call to our nation, divisions developed along racial lines. These divisions eventually led to the founding of the Assemblies of God denomination for Caucasian people and the Church of God in Christ for African Americans.

Reacting to "privatistic faith" that seems to relegate God's power only to the relief of personal pain, Dr. Lewis Smedes makes this point:

> We need to pray for power encounters between Christ and the devil in the matrix of devilish political systems. It seems to me that the big battlefield is in the systems that determine the lives of millions of people at a crack. . . . We are part of a fairly benign social system that still turns helpless people out into the streets, homeless, hopeless. Where is the power encounter here? We must howl against it in decibels that can drown out all the hosannas for the healing of well-housed Americans when

their bourgeois bursitis miraculously goes away. . . . I do not see how the gospel can vindicate itself to the suffering world if we celebrate occasional releases of individuals from bearable aches and pains while we are not much burdened by the people who suffer under the oppression of demonic systems.
—"What's Wrong with Celebrating a Miracle?" *The Reformed Journal*, Vol. 39, No. 2, Feb. 14-21, 1989, p. 20.

REFORMED EVANGELISM: PERSONAL AND CORPORATE

At a recent gathering of a Church Multiplication Alliance in New York City, Dr. Tim Keller of Redeemer Presbyterian Church gave a talk titled "A Vision for New York." He reflected on how New York is probably the most influential city in the world and challenged us to image how doubling the number of Bible-believing Christians could transform New York and through New York the world. Keller proposed that this transformation would not come through the planting of just any kind of church or the conversion of just any kind of Christian. It would come through those who are evangelizing, living in true community, ministering in word and deed, integrating faith and work, and continuing to multiply new churches. He added,

Culture is changed not simply through the accumulation of changed lives, but by Christians uniting to work across vocational fields—academia, business, the arts, media—in strategic culture-producing centers such as New York City.

Robert Linthicum identifies four marks of effective ministry. Those who attempt to do Reformed evangelism would do well to answer his four questions:

▸ Are the systems of a city being confronted and offered real potential for change?
▸ Are the poor and exploited of the city provided the vehicles by which they can bring about change in their situation?
▸ Are the middle class and the powerful given the opportunity to join in common cause with the poor to confront the systems of the city and seek their transformation?
▸ Is there a spiritual transformation going on in that city, or are the changes only social? Are the lives both of that city's poor and of its powerful being changed by God?
—*City of God—City of Satan: A Biblical Theology of the Urban Church*, Zondervan Publishing House, 1991, p. 193.

A biblically Reformed understanding of the gospel recognizes the need for personal and structural change without creating a dichotomy between spiritual and social structures. As we have seen from history, the conversion of individual believers alone does not change corrupt systems and structures.

Too often Christianity has simply caved in to the status quo and lost its prophetic edge. On the other hand, too often social justice has lost the heart of the gospel in its relationship with Christ. This has led to a world of institutions that began with Christian roots, desiring to bring Christ's transformation to education, health care, youth, but that are now secular universities or social service agencies, no different from any other. Too often the Reformed approach to the powers has not recognized them as possessed by personal spiritual beings, and battles have been fought against "flesh and blood" instead of against "principalities and powers."

BRINGING SOCIETAL AND STRUCTURAL CHANGE

CALLED TO CONFESSION

One of the first steps toward bringing about structural change is confession and repentance. Many Christians are not even aware of their participation in structural sin. I can still remember the moment when the Christian Reformed Church in North America identified the apartheid of South Africa as sin and its theological justification as heresy. We chastised our brothers and sisters of our sister denomination for continuing to endorse it and broke fellowship with them until they abolished it. More recently, we have adopted statements and taken steps toward eliminating racism from our own denominational agencies and local church.

In 1996, over 40,000 pastors gathered in Atlanta for the Promise Keepers Pastors' Conference. At one point, Coach Mac made confession of sin to pastors of color on behalf of the sins of the "white" church. As he invited them forward to be honored, spontaneous applause broke out, and leaders began embracing each other and confessing their sin to each other. Confession and repentance calls us to recognize the structural as well as the personal sin that we often participate in without even realizing it.

In his classic work on the biblical integration of evangelism, discipleship, and social justice, Waldron Scott challenges Christians to be "doers of the Word." Scott calls us to confession and repentance of our corporate sin in these words:

> The Apostle Peter declares boldly, "The time has come for judgment to begin with the household of God" (1 Peter 4:17). Each one of us, as members of a church or para-church organization, has a moral obligation to ask whether our own institution practices justice or whether our Christian bodies are molded instead after worldly corporations whose practices promote global injustice.
> —*Bring Forth Justice,* William B. Eerdmans Publishing Co., 1980, p. 257.

CALLED TO PRAYER

Applying the principles of this book to the structures of our age also calls us to prayer. In his book *Concerts of Prayer* (Regal Books, 1984, p. 131), David Bryant recommends praying for the overthrow of oppressive governments; the strengthening of just governments; and an end to war, hunger, nuclear proliferation, and economic oppression. He emphasizes,

> Solidarity praying calls us to pray with a desire that every dimension of the new heaven and the new earth may be brought to pass. As we pray for specific kingdom concerns for our world—such as justice, peace, reconciliation, and wholeness—we should do so with words that anticipate a full break through of God's kingdom. We should want all of what God wants, and be willing to say so— now!

This anticipation of "a full break through of God's kingdom" calls for

- profound prayer to uphold Christian politicians who are the presence of Christ in the midst of demon-possessed systems.
- prayer-walking the halls of our capital, statehouses, city halls, courthouses, and other places of power.
- initiating prayer with economic movers and shakers, politicians, judges, police chiefs, public school superintendents, and all who are in places of power and influence.

Our local clergy group now makes it a practice to lay hands on and pray over all politicians who come and want to speak to us. We pray for truth, honesty, righteousness, a public servant's heart, and that any violations of oaths of office will lead to their removal. Pastor Stafford Miller, my prayer partner and best friend, has recently been asked to lead in prayer before school prayer-walks in a local public school.

Whether on the streets of our hometowns, in urban cities around our nation, or in countries across the globe, prayer must accompany the power of the gospel in action.

THY KINGDOM COME

A biblical theology of the kingdom of God provides the foundation for us to expect the continued and daily involvement of a sovereign God, ruling Christ, and empowering Spirit to bring about personal and structural change. A Reformed theology and worldview stresses the need for Christians, both individually and corporately, to influence institutions in the name of Christ.

God's kingdom is established through one Christian caring for one person in need, visiting one hurting neighbor, or leading one person to Christ. The kingdom is also established through Christian political parties, lobby groups, labor unions, psychiatric and health care facilities, ministries to the poor, Christian schools, adoption agencies, relief and housing organizations. In Reformed circles, these are often called "kingdom ministries" to acknowledge their roots in a theology of the present kingdom of God. All of these ministries attempt to address their area of concern in a distinctively Christian way, under the lordship of Christ and from a kingdom perspective. These ministries are signs and wonders of God's kingdom. In addition, many Christians are involved in a multitude of ways in transforming educational, criminal justice, economic, political, and religious structures in the name of Christ.

The combining of a personal Christian witness and corporate Christian proclamation is beautifully illustrated by Wilma and Juanita, two former members of my congregation. Neighbors, prayer partners, and friends, they have sought to be a transforming influence in their small corner of the city of Paterson. They each purchased and repaired homes on North Fourth Street. This small spark of neighborhood renovation continued to spread up the street. Together they prayed weekly for personal healing and healing in their neighborhood and city; for the young men selling crack on the corner, and for the eradication of drug abuse from the city;

for the Christians on the block, and for the conversions of those who are unbelievers.

As strong leaders for the neighborhood organization, this new family reaches out to the children of the block and holds a weekly neighborhood Bible study for adults. They petition the city council for neighborhood services and participate in prayer marches throughout the community. Their witness is personal and corporate and includes proclamation and demonstration. Their confrontation of the powers is in prayer and presence, in humble service and powerful confrontation, in quiet acts of love and loud demonstrations of protest.

May that be said of us all.

CONCLUSION

Together, we've covered a lot of ground. We've learned that

- signs point to something beyond themselves.
- wonders cause us to stop and say WOW!
- miracles are works of power beyond ourselves.

The signs, wonders, and miracles that God chooses to do today may be the same as or different from what they were 2,000 or 3,000 years ago. Yet we have seen that God works in response to his people's prayers and obedience. The apostle Paul reminds us that God "is able to do immeasurably more than all we ask or imagine," but that he often chooses to do so "according to his power that is at work within us" (Eph. 3:20).

God gives us power (dunamis), and Jesus gives us authority (Matt. 28:18-20) to pray down demonic strongholds in our communities, nation, and world. This requires identifying and confronting the powers and recognizing their sinful and demonic natures. This also requires corporate confession and persistent prayer. The transformation of "principalities and powers" comes through the conversion of individual believers as well as through engaging believers in daily spiritual battles against the world, the flesh, and the devil's economic, political, cultural, educational, social, and entertainment strongholds.

The purpose of God's miracles, signs, and wonders in transforming these systems is to

- proclaim the Word of God.
- demonstrate the presence of the kingdom of God.
- demonstrate the power of the Holy Spirit.
- testify to the power of prayer.
- ground our faith in Jesus.
- defeat the devil.

Transformation happens through the power of the Holy Spirit, through confession and prayer, and through the power of faithful Christian witness that is itself a sign and wonder. In the words of the hymn with which we began this chapter, "with deeds of love and mercy, the heavenly kingdom comes."

> Then I saw a new heaven and a new earth, for the first heaven and the first earth had passed away, and there was no longer any sea. I saw the Holy City, the new Jerusalem, coming down out of heaven from God, prepared as a bride beautifully dressed for her husband. And I heard a loud voice from the throne saying, "Now the dwelling of God is with men, and he will live with them. They will be his people, and God himself will be with them and be their God. He will wipe every tear from their eyes. There will be no more death or mourning or crying or pain, for the old order of things has passed away." He who was seated on the throne said, "I am making everything new!"
>
> —Revelation 21:1-5

TESTIMONIES FROM . . .

THE BRITISH EMPIRE (1833)

In 1833 slave owners in the British Empire were commanded to release their slaves in one year's time. . . . One of the most important means used to attain this result was prayer. The Clapham leaders habitually spent three separate hours in prayer daily, and Christians all over England united in prayer on the eve of the critical debates. Other means used included ceaseless publicizing of the evils of slavery, the gathering of petitions from all over the country, and even the boycott of slave-produced goods. . . . It is inconceivable that the work could have been accomplished without a broad base of popular sentiment supplied by conversions and awakening throughout the English churches.

—Richard R. Lovelace, *Dynamics of Spiritual Life*, InterVarsity Press, 1979, pp. 370-371.

MARTIN LUTHER KING, JR. (1963)

It was a Sunday afternoon, when several hundred Birmingham Negroes had determined to hold a prayer meeting near the city jail. They gathered at the New Pilgrim Baptist Church and began an orderly march. Bull Connor ordered out the police dogs and fire hoses. When the marchers approached the border between the white and Negro areas, Connor ordered them to turn back. . . . We asked everybody to get down on their knees. Somebody just started praying in these old traditional chants of the black community (the theological dynamic). People were moaning, crying and praying. . . . All of a sudden some old lady got up and said, "God is with this movement, we goin' on to the jail." She got up and everybody started . . . (getting up). Enraged, Bull Connor whirled on his men and shouted ". . . Turn on the hoses." What happened in the next thirty seconds was one of the most fantastic events of the Birmingham story. These firemen . . . who really didn't know any better, had been so moved by this experience that they never turned the hoses on. Connor's men, as though hypnotized, fell back, their hoses sagging uselessly in their hands while several hundred Negros marched past them. The dogs that had been straining at the leash, jumping at us, all of a sudden just stopped, and we walked right on through. And somebody hollered out, "Great God Almighty done parted the Red Sea one more time."

—Carl Ellis, *Beyond Liberation*, InterVarsity Press, 1983, pp. 70-71.

ROBERT C. LINTHICUM (1991)

When reconciliation or negotiations with oppressive systems and their people fail, a community must respond through confrontation. To confront the principalities and powers, one must first understand them (after all, the first rule of warfare is "Know your enemy"). One gains understanding of his enemy through a power analysis. . . . The community organization with which I worked in Chicago became aware that banks, insurance companies and other fiduciary institutions had "red lined" our two communities. Red-lining is when corporations determine together to approve no loans, only offer insurance with extremely exorbitant premium payments, and otherwise make it difficult for people to maintain their homes and for firms to do business in the community. . . . We began a power analysis of the institutions involved. The evidence soon mounted in convincing volume, and our power analysis of each participating institution soon made it clear that the most vulnerable of those institutions to public pressure were the banks. . . . We also discovered that the churches in the community had major investments in those banks. Through those churches, we could reach about sixty percent of all the people living in the community. Our power analysis, therefore, gave us our strategy. . . . We got signed affidavits from them that each institution and individual would withdraw funds at our command, thus risking a "run" on the bank. We met with the bank president and, backed with these affidavits, got the bank to reverse its lending policies. . . . With the withdrawal of that bank from the scheme, the attempted red-lining of that community quickly collapsed.

—*City of God—City of Satan: A Biblical Theology of the Urban Church,*
Zondervan Publishing House, 1991, pp. 214.

CHARLES COLSON (1990)

In their high expectations of politics, many Christians also misjudge the source of true societal reform. In reality, it is impossible to effect genuine political reform without reforming individual and, eventually, national character. While it has a moral responsibility to restrain evil, government can never change the hearts and minds of its citizens. Attitudes are forged by spiritual forces, not by legislation. "All history, once you strip the rind off the kernel, is really spiritual," said historian Arnold Toynbee. Values change when spiritual movements stir the hearts of people and when fresh winds of reason stir their minds. . . . Not that I advocate withdrawal from politics. I believe every aspect of life is subject to Christ's lordship and that Christians are called to bring biblical influence to every part of society, including political structures. That's my objective when I speak before state legislatures and other political groups, urging reforms in our criminal justice system. We are to work within and without politics for justice and righteousness.

—*Against the Night,* Servant Publications, 1989, pp. 118-119.

REFORMED REFLECTIONS

OUR WORLD BELONGS TO GOD: A CONTEMPORARY TESTIMONY, STANZAS 44 AND 56

Following the apostles, the church is sent—
sent with the gospel of the kingdom
to make disciples of all nations,
to feed the hungry,
and to proclaim the assurance that in the name of Christ
there is forgiveness of sin and new life
for all who repent and believe—
to tell the news that our world belongs to God.
In a world estranged from God,
where millions face confusing choices,
this mission is central to our being,
for we announce the one name that saves.
We repent of leaving this work to a few,
we pray for brothers and sisters

who suffer for the faith,
and we rejoice that the Spirit
is waking us to see
our mission in God's world.

Our hope for a new earth is not tied
to what humans can do,
for we believe that one day
every challenge to God's rule
and every resistance to his will shall be crushed.
Then his kingdom shall come fully
and our Lord shall rule forever.

> Reflect on some current challenges
> "to God's rule" and "resistance to his will."

QUESTIONS TO THINK ABOUT

▸ What are some specific rulers, authorities, powers, and spiritual forces of evil that you see working against the kingdom of God today?

▸ What are some ways that you can confront these powers in the name of Christ?

▸ How have you been, or can you be, a "sign" of Christ and the presence of his kingdom in addressing the following structures?
  - politics
  - racism
  - oppression
  - peacemaking
  - education
  - economics
  - earthkeeping
  - other (specify)

PRAYER AND PRACTICE

Pray aloud these prayers from the book of Revelation:

To him who loves us
and has freed us from our sins by his blood,
and has made us to be a kingdom and priests
to serve his God and Father—
to him be glory and power for ever and ever! Amen (1:5-6).

"You are worthy, our Lord and God,
to receive glory and honor and power,
for you created all things,
and by your will they were created
and have their being" (4:11).

"You are worthy to take the scroll
and to open its seals,
because you were slain,
and with your blood you purchased men for God
from every tribe and language and people and nation.
You have made them to be a kingdom and priests
to serve our God,
and they will reign on the earth" (5:9-10).

"Worthy is the Lamb, who was slain,
to receive power and wealth and wisdom and strength
and honor and glory and praise!" (5:12).

"To him who sits on the throne and to the Lamb
be praise and honor and glory and power,
for ever and ever!" (5:13).

"Hallelujah!
Salvation and glory and power
belong to our God" (19:1).

Confess your involvement in corporate sins of racism, oppression, pollution, greed, selfishness, and more. Practice James's advice: "confess your sins to each other and pray for each other so that you may be healed" (5:16).

ADDITIONAL RESOURCES

BOOKS

▸ Berkhof, Hendrik. *Christ and the Powers.* Translated by John H. Yoder. Scottdale, Penn.: Herald Press, 1962.

▸ Linthicum, Robert C. *City of God—City of Satan: A Biblical Theology of the Urban Church.* Grand Rapids, Mich.: Zondervan Publishing House, 1991.

DVD

▸ Otis Jr., George. *The Quickening: Entering into the Firestorm of God's Grace.* The Sentinel Group, Global Net Productions, 2003. www.transformnations.com.

ORGANIZATIONS/MOVEMENTS

▸ The Micah Challenge: A Global Christian Campaign. Aims to deepen our engagement with the poor and to challenge leaders to achieve the Millennium Development Goals and so to halve absolute global poverty by 2015. www.Micahchallenge.org.

▸ The Center for Public Justice (formerly APJ). Mission: Serve God, advance justice, transform public life. www.cpjustice.org.

▸ Evangelicals for Social Action. *Prism* (bimonthly magazine). www.esa-online.org.